שָׁלוֹם וּבְרָכָה

The New Hebrew Primer

Pearl Tarnor • Carol Levy

T0017861

BEHRMAN HOUSE

לשמואל יחזקאל

מסבתא

לקובי ורעה

מאמא

ושננתם לבניך

"And you shall teach them diligently to your children."

Activities by Roberta Osser Baum, Rae Eskin, and Aviva Lucas Gutnick

Editorial consultants: Ellen Rank, Terry Kaye

Special thanks to Danielle Greene for creating the Hebrew files for the revised edition
and to Judy Sandman for proofreading the revised edition.

Artwork by: Joni Levy Liberman (chapter openers); Deborah Zemke (activity art)

Published by Behrman House, Inc.
Millburn, New Jersey 07041
www.behrmanhouse.com

ISBN 978-1-68115-156-4

Library of Congress Control Number: 2023950825

Design by Zatar Creative
Revised edition project manager: Aviva Lucas Gutnick
Original edition project manager: Terry Kaye

Printed in China

1 3 5 7 9 8 6 4 2

TABLE OF CONTENTS

שַׁבָּת

Shabbat

NEW LETTERS

שׁ	ת	בּ

NEW VOWELS

ָ	ַ

BET

ָ	ַ

1   בַּ   בַּ   בַּ   בַּ   בַּ   בַּ

2   בָּ   בָּ   בָּ   בָּ   בָּ   בָּ

3   בָּ   בַּ   בָּ   בַּ   בַּ   בָּ

4   בָּ בַּ בָּ   בָּ בַּ בָּ   בַּ בָּ בַּ   בָּ בַּ בָּ

SHAPE IT UP

What does **Bet** look like?
Close your eyes and picture the letter.
Draw it in the air or use your whole body
to make the shape of the letter **Bet**.

Make up a clue to remember **Bet**.

What do  sound like?

Make a hand motion to show
the shape of ַ and ָ as
you say their sound.

4

I SPY

Read aloud each line.

Find the sound that's different from the others.

Circle it or highlight it.

בּ בּ	בּ בּ	בַּ	בּ בּ	בּ בּ	בּ בּ	1
בָּ	בָּ	בָּ	בּ	בָּ	בָּ	2
בּ	בּ	בּ	בּ	בֵּ	בּ	3
בֵּ	בֵּ	בּ	בֵּ	בֵּ	בֵּ	4

SOUNDS LIKE

Clap your hands as you read aloud each line. Which two Hebrew sounds are the same? Circle them or tell a partner.

בֵּ	בּ	בֵּ	1
בּ	בֵּ	בּ	2
בָּ	בָּ	בּ	3

בּ בּ	בָּ	בָּ	4
בּ בּ	בֵּ	בּ	5
בֵּ בּ	בּ	בָּ	6

תֵּ	תֵּ	תָּ	תַּ	תָּ	תַּ	1
תּ	תַּ	תָּ	תּ	תַּ	תָּ	2

TAV

SHAPE IT UP

What does **Tav** look like? Close your eyes and picture the letter. Draw it in the air or use your whole body to make the shape of the letter **Tav**.

Make up a clue to remember **Tav**.

HEADS UP!

The letters תּ and ת make the same sound.

Say that sound aloud.

Read each line below softly. Read the lines again loudly.

תַּ	תָּ	תְּ	ב	בַּ	תַּ	1
בַּ	תַּ	תָּ	ת	ב	בָּ	2
תַּת	תַּבַּ	תָּבְּ	תָּת	תָּתָ	תַת	3
תַּב	בַּת	תַּבַּ	בַּת	תַּב	תָּבָ	4
בַּת	תַּב	בָּב	תָּב	בָּתָ	בַּת	5
בַּת בָּתָ בַּבַּ	בָּתְ	תָּבְב	בַּתָת	תָּבָת	6

Great job!

EXTRA CREDIT

How many times did you read the Hebrew word for *daughter*?

_____

I KNOW HEBREW!

Can you find this Hebrew word above?

daughter = בַּת

Read and circle or highlight it.

WORD RIDDLE

I am written on a scroll. I am kept in the Ark. I am read in the synagogue.

My name begins with the letter ת.

What am I?

I SPY

Read aloud each line.

Find the sound that's different from the others. Jump up and say the name of that letter..

בּ   בּ   בּ   ⟨תּ⟩   בּ   בּ   **1**

תּ   בּ   תּ   תּ   תּ   תּ   **2**

בּ   בּ   בּ   בּ   בּ   תּ   **3**

תּ   תּ   בּ   תּ   תּ   תּ   **4**

בּ   תּ   תּ   תּ   תּ   תּ   **5**

בּ   בּ   בּ   בּ   תּ   בּ   **6**

SHIN

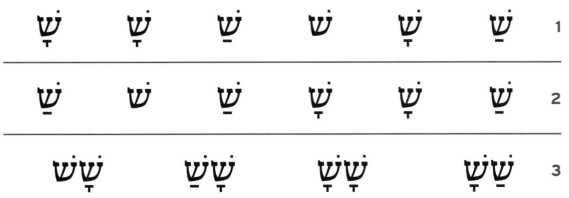

שָׁ   שָׁ   שַׁ   שַׁ   שָׁ   שַׁ   **1**

שִׁ   שִׁ   שִׁ   שָׁ   שָׁ   שִׁ   **2**

שָׁשִׁ   שָׁשַׁ   שַׁשִׁ   שָׁשַׁ   **3**

SHAPE IT UP

What does *Shin* look like?

Close your eyes and picture the letter. Draw it in the air or use your whole body to make the shape of the letter *Shin*.

Make up a clue to remember *Shin*.

READY, SET, READ

Read the lines below as fast as you can. Try to read them again even faster!

1	בָּ	בַּ	בּ	בֵּ	בְּ	בְּ
2	תָּ	תַּ	תּ	תָּ	תַּ	תּ
3	שָׁשׁ	שַׁבּ	שָׁתּ	שָׁשׁ	שָׁבּ	שָׁתָּ
4	בַּשׁ	תָּשׁ	בַּתּ	שַׁתּ	בָּשָׁ	בַּתּ
5	שָׁבַשׁ	תָּשַׁבּ	תַּבָּשׁ	תַּבַּתּ	בַּשָׁתּ
6	שַׁבַּבּ	בַּתָּבּ	תָּתַבּ	בַּבָּתּ	תַּבַּתּ
7	תָּבָּתּ	שַׁבַּתָּ	בַּשָׁתּ	בָּשָׁשׁ	בַּבָּתּ
8	שַׁבָּתּ	שַׁבָּתּ	שַׁבָּתּ	שַׁבָּתּ	שַׁבָּתּ

I KNOW HEBREW!

Can you find this Hebrew word above?

Shabbat = שַׁבָּת

Read and circle or highlight it.

EXTRA CREDIT

God created the world in six days. On the seventh day God rested.

Which line contains the name of that special day?

_____

8

I SPY

Read aloud each line.

Find the Hebrew that sounds the same as the English in the box.

Circle it or sing it out loud.

שָׁ	ב	תּ	תַּ	(בַּ)	שֹׁ	BAH	1
ב	תּ	תָּ	שָׁ	שׁ	בָּ	TAH	2
ב	שָׁ	בָּ	תַּ	שׁ	בֵּ	B	3
בַּ	ב	תַּ	שָׁ	שׁ	ת	SHAH	4
שׁ	בָּ	תָּ	שׁ	תַּ	ת	T	5
שַׁ	שׁ	ב	ת	תָּ	שָׁ	SH	6

CONNECTIONS

Connect each Hebrew letter to its name.

What sound does each letter make?

SHIN

TAV

BET

TAV

בַּ

תּ שׁ

תּ

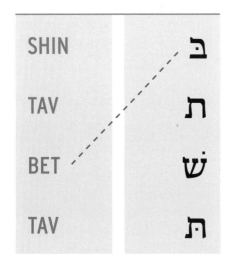

HEADS UP!

Bet (ב) makes the sound _____.

Tav (תּ or ת) makes the sound _____.

Shin (שׁ) makes the sound _____.

What do you notice about the names of these Hebrew letters and the sounds the letters make?

בּ   בּ   בּ

ת   ת   תּ   ת

שׁ   שׁ   שׁ

Write the Hebrew word for **daughter**.

בַּת   בַּת   בַּת

Write the Hebrew word for **Shabbat**.

שַׁבָּת   שַׁבָּת

MAKE A MATCH

What is the name of each letter?

Write the letter on the line.

ת	SHIN	TAV	BET	תּ	1
	BET	SHIN	TAV	בּ	2
	TAV	BET	SHIN	שׁ	3
	SHIN	BET	TAV	ת	4

OUR TRADITION — שַׁבָּת

שַׁבָּת means "rest."
God created the world in six days.
On the seventh day, God rested.
We call that special day שַׁבָּת.

How do you rest and relax?
Draw a picture of yourself doing that.

WELCOMING שַׁבָּת

On Friday evening when Shabbat begins, we welcome it with blessings and songs.

Write the word שַׁבָּת on the line below each object we use to welcome שַׁבָּת.

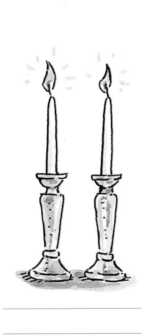

שֶׁמֶשׁ

Helper

NEW LETTER

מ

LETTERS YOU KNOW. Say the name and sound of each letter.

שׁ ת תּ ב

VOWELS YOU KNOW. Say the sound of each vowel.

ָ ַ

מַ	מ	מָ	מ	מָ	מַ 1
שָׁ	מָ	תָּ	ת	ב	מַ 2
שׁ	מָ	שָׁ	שׁ	מָ	מַ 3

MEM

מ

SHAPE IT UP

What does **Mem** look like?

Close your eyes and picture the letter.

Draw it in the air or use your whole body to make the shape of the letter **Mem**.

Make up a clue to remember **Mem**.

Read the first two lines s-l-o-w-l-y. Read them again correctly as fast as you can.
Take turns with a partner reading every other line at a regular pace.

בָּת	שַׁבָּ	מְשׁ	מָמְ	מַמָ	מָשׁ	שָׁמָ	1
מַבְ	מַתָּ	מַמַ	מָת	מַב	מָשׁ	2
תַמַ	בָּמְ	בַת	תָּמְ	שָׁמָ	בַּמַ	3
בָּמְשׁ	מַמַת	מַבַּת	מַתְשׁ	מְשַׁב	4
מָשַׁשׁ	מַבָּשׁ	תַמַת	שַׁבָּת	תָּמַשׁ	5
שַׁמְשׁ	מָשַׁשׁ	מָתְשׁ	שָׁמְשׁ	שַׁבָּת	6
שָׁמְשׁ	שַׁבָּת	שַׁבְּ	שָׁמְשׁ	שָׁמָ	7
שַׁבָּת	שָׁמְשׁ	שַׁבָּת	שָׁמְשׁ	שַׁבָּת	8

I KNOW HEBREW!

Can you find this Hebrew word above?
helper candle on the hanukkiyah,
the Hanukkah menorah = שַׁמָּשׁ

Read it, then circle or point to it
each time you find it.

EXTRA CREDIT

How many times did you
read the word for **helper**?

_____

13

I SPY

Find the English that sounds the same as the Hebrew in the box.

Circle it or sing it out loud.

(T)	M	B	SH	ת	1
MAH	SHAH	SH	TAH	שָׁ	2
M	TAH	MAH	BAH	מָ	3
MAH	SH	TAH	SHAH	שׁ	4
BAH	T	B	TAH	בָּ	5

WORD RIDDLE

You eat me on Passover. I am flat and crunchy. My name begins with the letter מ. What am I?

Draw a picture of me with your favorite topping or tell a partner about your favorite topping for me.

WRITING PRACTICE

מָא

Write the Hebrew word for **helper**.

שָׁמָשׁ

Write the Hebrew word for **Shabbat**.

שָׁבָּת

How did you do? Circle your best **Mem** above.

OUR TRADITION — שַׁמָשׁ

שַׁמָשׁ means "helper." The שַׁמָשׁ is the helper candle on the **hanukkiyah**, the Hanukkah menorah.

We use the שַׁמָשׁ to light the other candles.

What do you think is special about using a שַׁמָשׁ to light a Hanukkah menorah?

CONNECTIONS

Say the sound of each letter.

Match each letter to the picture whose name begins with the same sound.

שׁ

מ

ת

NAME THAT LETTER

Write the Hebrew letter under its name.

SHIN	BET	TAV	MEM
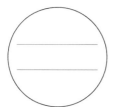	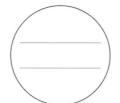	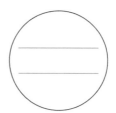	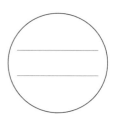

כַּלָה
Bride

LETTERS YOU KNOW. Say the name and sound of each letter.

בּ תּ שׁ ת מ

VOWELS YOU KNOW. Say the sound of each vowel.

ָ ־

NEW LETTERS

ל כּ ה

LAMED

ל

לַ	ל	לְ	ל	לְ	לַ	1
מ	מָ מַ	מַ	ל	לַ	לְ	2
תָ	מָ	שַׁ	תַּ	בָּ	לְ	3

SHAPE IT UP

What does **Lamed** look like? Close your eyes and picture the letter.
Draw it in the air or use your whole body to make the
shape of the letter **Lamed**.

Make up a clue to remember **Lamed**.

16

Read the odd-numbered lines to a partner. Have a partner read the even-numbered lines to you.

שׁ	שָׁ	בַּ	בְ	תַּ	תְ	1
תַּל	שַׁל	לָת	לְשׁ	מַמָ	לַמָ	2
לַבּ	לָל	לַת	לְשָׁ	לְמָ	לַת	3
מַל	תַּל	שָׁל	בַּל	לָל	שָׁמָ	4
מַמָשׁ	מַלָת	בָּלַת	שָׁלָשׁ	בַּת		5
מָלַל	לַבַּת	תָּלַל	מָשָׁל	מָלַל		6
בַּלָשׁ	שָׁמָשׁ	תָּלַשׁ	שָׁלָל	לַמָשׁ		7
שָׁמָשׁ	לַשָׁמָשׁ	שָׁבָת	לַשַׁבָּת	שָׁמָשׁ		8

BONUS

Choose any word for a partner to read. Then have a partner choose any word for you to read. Continue until you've each read four words. Challenge each other with the long words!

EXTRA CREDIT

How many times did you read the word for **helper**? _____

How many times did you read the word for **daughter**? _____

SOUNDS LIKE

Read aloud each word on line 1.

Circle the Hebrew sounds that are the same.

Show a partner and have your partner read them.

Repeat for the other lines.

מֵשׁ	מָשָׁ	שָׁמַ	מֵשׁ	1
שַׁל	שָׁל	שָׁלַ	לָשׁ	2
תַּב	בָּ	בַּת	בַּתָ	3
לְבַּ	לַב	בְּל	לָב	4
מַל	לָמְ	לַמַ	לָל	5

I SPY

Read aloud each line.

Find and circle the Hebrew that sounds the same as the English in the box.

בַּ	לַ	שׁ	תַּ	ל	LAH	1
ל	בַ	ת	מ	מָ	M	2
מ	תַּ	מַ	בַּ	שַׁ	MAH	3
ת	לַ	ב	שׁ	ל	L	4
מ	בַּ	שׁ	בַּ	שַׁ	SHAH	5

KAF

כ

כ	כַ	כָ	כ	כָ	כַ	1
מַ	שׁ	ת	ל	בָּ	כַ	2
מַ	כַ	בָּ	ת	כַ	בָּ	3

18

Read each line as s-l-o-w-l-y as you can. Read again only the sounds or words that have a **Lamed**.
Then read only the sounds or words that start with a **Kaf**.

כַּ	כְ	כ	בָּ	בַּ	ב	1
כַּשָׁ	כַּת	כָּשׁ	כָּמָ	כָּל	כַּבּ	2
כָּל	שָׁכַ	בַּכָּ	תַּכַּ	מַכָּ	לָכָ	3
בַּת	מָכָּ	שָׁמָ	תַּכַּ	בַּל	לָמָ	4
תַּכַּת	כָּלָל	כַּלָשׁ	מַכַּת	כַּבַּת		5
בָּלָת	כָּשַׁל	כָּתַשׁ	כָּלָל	כַּלָת		6
מַמָשׁ	שַׁבָּת	שַׁבָּת	שַׁמָשׁ	שָׁמָשׁ		7
כַּשָׁבָּת	כַּשַׁבָּת	שַׁבָּת	לַשַׁבָּת	שַׁבָּת		8

SHAPE IT UP

What does **Kaf** look like? Close your eyes and picture the letter.
Draw it in the air or use your whole body to make the shape of the letter **Kaf**.

Make up a clue to remember **Kaf**.

LETTER BOXES

Say the name of the letter in each box. Circle or point to the sound each letter makes. Say the sound.

T	SH	**3**	T	SH	**2**	B	L	**1**
מ			שׁ			בּ		
L	M		M	L		SH	M	

H	B	**6**	T	M	**5**	M	T	**4**
כּ			ל			ת		
L	K		L	B		SH	B	

הָ	ה	הַ	ה	הָ	הַ	**1**	**HAY**
הָ	שַׁ	מְ	לְ	כַּ	הַ	**2**	
הָ	שִׁ	הָ	הַ	מְ	הַ	**3**	

SHAPE IT UP

What does **Hay** look like?
Close your eyes and picture the letter.
Draw it in the air or use your whole body to
make the shape of the letter **Hay**.

Make up a clue to remember **Hay**.

HEADS UP!

The letter ה is pronounced "h,"
but when ה comes at the end of the
word and has no vowel under it,
it is silent.

READY, SET, READ

Find and read all the sounds and words that start with a **Hay**. Then read all the sounds and words that end with a **Hay**. Find and read all the sounds and words that do not have a **Hay**.

Which sound made you laugh? (Hint: it's on line 2.)

הָ	כַּ	הַ	תָּ	הָ	בַּ	1
הָהָ	הָת	הָשׁ	הַת	הָב	הַל	2
הַה	מָה	לָה	שָׁה	תָּה	בָּה	3
שַׁבָּת	כָּמָה	לָשָׁה	בָּמָה	תָּלָה		4
לָשָׁה	כָּלָב	שָׁמָב	מַכָּה	לָמָה		5
הַכַּלָה	הַמָּשָׁל	הַשַּׁבָּת	הַשֶּׁמֶשׁ	הַבַּת		6
לָשָׁה	לָמָה	כָּמָה	מַכָּה	הַכַּלָה	כַּלָה	7
שַׁבָּת הַכַּלָה		שַׁבָּת הַכַּלָה		שַׁבָּת הַכַּלָה		8

I KNOW HEBREW!

Can you find these Hebrew words above?

the Sabbath bride = שַׁבָּת הַכַּלָה

bride = כַּלָה

Read and circle or highlight them.

EXTRA CREDIT

How many times did you read the words for **Sabbath bride**?

_____

21

ל ל

כּ כּ

ה ה

Write the Hebrew word for **bride**.

כַּלָה

Write the Hebrew words for the **Sabbath bride**.

שַׁבָּת הַכַּלָה

How did you do? ☺ ☹

I SPY

Read each line.

Circle or highlight the English that sounds the same as the Hebrew letter in the box.

Write the Hebrew letter on the line or tell a partner the name of the letter.

שׁ	V	H	(SH)	T	שׁ	1
	SH	K	M	B	כּ	2
	L	G	H	S	ל	3
	M	SH	T	H	ה	4
	B	S	K	SH	בּ	5
	H	S	T	L	תּ	6
	SH	M	H	T	מ	7

OUR TRADITION — כַּלָה

Every Friday evening as we welcome שַׁבָּת, we say that שַׁבָּת is like a bride, כַּלָה.

Just as a כַּלָה is joyously welcomed at the wedding ceremony,
so we welcome שַׁבָּת with great happiness.

What are some ways that שַׁבָּת is like a כַּלָה?

WORD MATCH

Match each Hebrew term with its English meaning. Read each Hebrew-English match aloud.

BRIDE	שַׁבָּת
SABBATH	שֶׁמֶשׁ
HELPER	שַׁבָּת הַכַּלָה
THE SABBATH BRIDE	כַּלָה

ALEF BET CHART

You know these Hebrew letters:

ה כ ל מ שׁ ת תּ בּ

Turn to the **Alef Bet** chart on page 160. Color in the letters you have learned.

You will return to the chart again after a few more lessons.

The more letters you learn, the more colorful the **Alef Bet** chart will become.

בְּרָכָה

Blessing

LETTERS YOU KNOW. Say the name and sound of each letter.

ב ת תּ שׁ מ ל כ ה

VOWELS YOU KNOW. Say the sound of each vowel.

ָ   ַ

NEW LETTERS

כ   ר

NEW VOWEL

:

RESH

ר	רַ	רְ	רְ	רָ	רַ	1
כְּ	לְ	מְ	שְׁ	תְּ	בְּ	2
שְׁ	שָׁ	בַּ	בְּ	רְ	רַ	3

SHAPE IT UP

What does **Resh** look like?
Close your eyes and picture the letter.
Draw it in the air or use your whole body to make the shape of the letter **Resh**

Make up a clue to remember **Resh**.

What does : sound like?

Make a hand motion to show the

shape of : as you say its sound.

:

24

READY, SET, READ

Read aloud the lines below. Then read all the words with the ░ vowel. Remember, that vowel is often, but not always, silent. It makes a very short sound when it appears under the first letter in a word.

ל	לְ	מְ	מַ	ר	רַ	1
רַבְ	רַב	כְּרַ	שָׁרְ	כַּר	שָׁר	2
רָמְ	רְה	רַל	רַשׁ	רַת	רַב	3
הַר	כַּר	שָׁרְ	מַר	תַּר	בַּר	4
רָשַׁל	רָמָה	תָּשַׁר	כָּרָה	רַבָּה	5	
שָׁמַר	רַכָּה	שָׂרָה	מְרָה	הָרָה	6	
הַכָּרָה	שָׁרַת	שָׁמַר	שָׁמָשׁ	לְבַּר	רָשַׁל	7
שַׁבָּת הַמַּלְכָּה	הַכָּרָה	רָשְׁמָה	מַלְכָּה	שְׁמָרָה	8	

I KNOW HEBREW!

Can you find this Hebrew word above?
What line is it on?

queen = מַלְכָּה

Read the word the way you think a queen would read it. Don't forget to put on your (pretend) crown!

EXTRA CREDIT

Can you find the word for **helper**?

Write it here. _____

NAME TAG

Match the Hebrew with its name on each line. Say the sound of each letter.

HAY	(TAV)	SHIN	ת	1
SHIN	KAF	BET	בּ	2
RESH	HAY	TAV	ר	3
HAY	SHIN	BET	שׁ	4
KAF	HAY	TAV	ה	5
MEM	SHIN	LAMED	ל	6
LAMED	KAF	BET	כּ	7
MEM	LAMED	TAV	מ	8

CHAF

כִ	כָ	כ	כִ	כָ	כַ	1
כָ	כָ	כִ	כִ	כָ	בַ	2
בֵ	כ	כָ	בַ	כִ	כִ	3

HEADS UP!

The letters כ and כּ make different sounds.

What sound does כּ make?
What sound does כ make?

Practice making those two sounds.

SHAPE IT UP

What does **Chaf** look like?
Close your eyes and picture the letter.

Draw it in the air or use your whole body to make the shape of the letter **Chaf**.

Make up a clue to help you remember the difference between **Kaf** and **Chaf**.

READY, SET, READ

Read lines 1-4 in a happy 😊 voice. Read lines 5-8 in a sad 🙁 voice.

לְכָ	תָּכָ	רָכַ	כָּכַ	בְּכַ	מָכַ	1
כַשְׁ	כַּת	כַבָ	כָּכַ	מָכַ	כָה	2
בַּר	תַּכַ	כַר	שַׁכְ	כָמְ	רַכְ	3
כַּלַת	שָׁכַר	מָכַר	רַכָּה	כָּכָה	בָּכָה	4
לַכַּת	רָכַשׁ	מַכָּה	כַּמָה	כָהָה	כַלָה	5
לָכַשׁ	תָּכָה	לְכָה	כָּרָה	כָּכַת	בָּכַת	6
הָלַכְתָּ	מִכְרָה	כָּרַכְתָּ	הַתָּכָה	בָּכְתָה		7
מָשְׁכָה	הָלְכָה	בְּרָכָה	בְּרָכָה	הָלַכְתָּ		8

I KNOW HEBREW!

Can you find this Hebrew word above?

blessing = בְּרָכָה

How many times did you read the word for **blessing**?

_____

EXTRA CREDIT

Can you find a word above that sounds like another English word for automobile? (Hint: it's on line 3).

What Hebrew letters are in that word?

RHYME TIME

Read the Hebrew words in each column When you find two that rhyme, connect them and sing those words out loud.

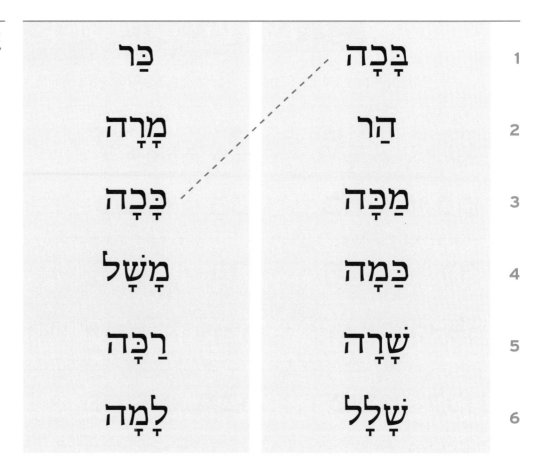

1	בָּכָה	כַּר
2	הַר	מָרָה
3	מַכָּה	כָּכָה
4	כַּמָה	מָשָׁל
5	שָׂרָה	רַכָּה
6	שָׁלָל	לָמָה

I SPY

Read aloud each line.

Find the sound that's different from the others. Circle or highlight it. Then, say the name of that letter.

1	ב	ב	ב	(ת)	ב	ב	ב
2	כ	ב	כ	כ	כ	כ	
3	ה	ת	ת	ת	ת	ת	
4	כ	כ	כ	כ	ת	כ	
5	ה	ה	ה	ה	ר	ה	ה
6	כ	כ	כ	כ	כ	כ	

ר ר→

כ כ→

Write the Hebrew word for **blessing**.

בְּרָכָה בְּרָכָה

Write the Hebrew word for **queen**.

מַלְכָּה מַלְכָּה

How did you do? Circle your best **Chaf** and your best **Resh** above.

ODD ONE OUT

Find the letter on each line that doesn't belong. Write it on the line.

בּ	ת	(ב)	ת	ת	ת	ת	1
	ה	ה	ר	ה	ה	ה	2
	שׁ	שׁ	שׁ	שׁ	ל	שׁ	3
	ת	ת	כ	ת	ת	4
	ת	ת	כ	ת	ת	5
	ב	ב	מ	ב	ב	ב	6

29

OUR TRADITION – בְּרָכָה

A בְּרָכָה is a blessing.

When we say a בְּרָכָה we praise God for the gifts God gives us.

For example, we praise God for the food we eat, for the Shabbat wine we drink, and even for a rainbow that stretches across the sky.

What do you praise or thank God for? Write it or draw it here.

WORDS YOU KNOW

Read each of the words below to a partner. Have your partner say the meaning of the word. Then switch. Do you know the meanings of all the words?

מַלְכָּה   בְּרָכָה   כַּלָה   שֶׁמֶשׁ   שַׁבָּת

EXTRA CREDIT

Can you use each Hebrew word in an English sentence?

Example: We welcome שַׁבָּת by lighting candles.

הַבְדָּלָה

Havdalah
Separation

LETTERS YOU KNOW. Say the name and sound of each letter.

כ ר ה כ ל מ שׁ ת ב

VOWELS YOU KNOW. Say the sound of each vowel.

_   ָ   ְ

NEW LETTERS

ב ד

NEW VOWEL

VET

ב

בְ	בַ	בְּ	בְּ	בָ	בַ	1
בְּ	בְּ	בַ	בַ	הַ	הֱ	2
ב	כ	בְּ	כְ	בַ	כַ	3

SHAPE IT UP

What does **Vet** look like?
Close your eyes and picture the letter.
Draw it in the air or use your whole body
to make the shape of the letter **Vet**.

Make up a clue to help you remember
the difference between **Vet** and **Bet**.

What does ⬚ sound like?
Make a hand motion to show the
shape of ⬚ as you say its sound.

31

READY, SET, READ

Read all the words that contain a **Bet**. Then read all the words that contain a **Vet**.
Find and read all the words that don't contain a **Bet** or a **Vet**.

שָׁב	הָב	רָב	תָּב	כָּב	בָּב	1
בַּת	כָּבֵ	הַב	מַבְּ	שָׁב	תָּבְ	2
הָבָ	מַב	בַּל	כָּב	רַב	לֵב	3
הָבָה	לָבַשׁ	כָּתַב	שָׁבָה	שָׁרַב	4
רָבָה	שָׁבַּר	רַבָּה	בָּבָה	לַבָּה	5
הַבְרָה	כָּתַבְתְּ	שָׁבַרְתְּ	רְבָבָה	לַבְלָר	6
כָּתְבָה	הַמְרָה	הָלְכָה	הָרְמָה	לְהָבָה	7
הָלְכָה	מְבַלָה	הַתָּרָה	הֲתַשָׁה	הַשָׁבָה	8

EXTRA CREDIT

Find the words that contain both a **Bet**
and a **Vet**.

How many words did you find? ____

HEADS UP!

The vowels ◻ָ , ◻ֱ , ◻ַ
make the same sound.

Say that sound.

WORD WIZARD

A word you've learned is hidden below.
Cross out the Hebrew letters and vowels that match the English sounds below.
Write the remaining Hebrew letters and their vowels on the lines below to discover the hidden word.

1	SHAH		4	HAH
2	V		5	K
3	LAH		6	T

תּ   ה   כְּ   כָ   הָ   רָ   לְ   בְּ   שַׁ

_____   _____   _____

What does the word mean? _____

ד	דְּ	דַ	דְ	דָ	דַ	1
דָ	כָ	רְ	דְ	רַ	הֶ	2
ר	ד	דָ	דָ	רַ	דַ	3

DALET

SHAPE IT UP

What does **Dalet** look like? Close your eyes and picture the letter.
Draw it in the air or use your whole body to make the shape of the letter **Dalet**.

Make up a clue to remember **Dalet**.

33

READY, SET, READ

Read aloud the odd-numbered lines below in a funny voice.
Read the even-numbered lines in your regular voice.

רֵשׁ	דֵּשׁ	בֵּר	בַּד	דָר	דָּד	1
דָּב	דָר	דָה	דַל	דַת	דָשׁ	2
רַד	הַד	שַׂדְ	בַּדְ	כַּד	מַד	3
דָרָה	הָדָר	לָמַד	דְּבַשׁ	דָּבָר	דָּלָה	4
לְבַד	דָהָה	דָרַשׁ	שָׂדַד	דָּשָׁה	מָדַד	5
הֶבְרָה	הַדְרָה	הֲלָכָה	דְּמָמָה	הֶמְרָה	6
מְדָדָה	דַּרְכְתָּ	לָמְדָה	לָבַשְׁתָּ	כָּתְבָה	7
הַבְדָּלָה	בְּרָכָה	הֲלָכָה	דְּרָשָׁה	הַבְדָּלָה	8

I KNOW HEBREW!

Can you find this Hebrew word above?

havdalah, separation = הַבְדָּלָה

Read it and circle or highlight it.

EXTRA CREDIT

How many times did you read
the word for *separation*?

_____

SOUNDS LIKE

Read the Hebrew in each box.

Then read the Hebrew on each line. When you hear a sound the same as the sound in the box, snap your fingers.

#	box			
1	הַבָ	תַבַ	הַבַ	הָךְ
2	בַּד	בָּדְ	בַּךְ	כַּד
3	רָשָׁה	דָשָׁה	רָתָה	רָשַׁ
4	כָּךְ	כַּךְ	בָּךְ	כַּבְ
5	דָבָר	דָבַה	רָבָךְ	דַבֵּר

I SPY

Find and read the Hebrew that sounds the same as the English in the box. Circle it or tell a partner.

#	box							
1	RAH	הַ	תַ	ר	ר	בְּ	וְ	דַ
2	KAH	הְַ	ה	כַּ	ב	כְ	כְּ	
3	V	בְּ	ב	תְ	ר	בַ	כַ	
4	D	דַ	כְ	וְ	דְ	רַ	ה	
5	HAH	רַ	הְַ	דַ	ה	מַ	תַ	
6	K	כְ	רְ	כַּ	בְּ	שׁ	כְּ	

35

בַּ בּ

דַ דּ

Write the Hebrew word for **havdalah, separation.**

הַבְדָלָה

Write the Hebrew word for **Shabbat.**

שַׁבָּת

How did you do? Circle your best **Vet** and your best **Dalet** above.

NAME TAG

Read aloud the name of the Hebrew letter in each box. Find its matching Hebrew letter and write it on the line.

ל	ה	ד	(ל)	מ	LAMED	1
	ת	ה	ב	ר	HAY	2
	כ	ת	ד	בּ	VET	3
	מ	ל	כ	שׁ	MEM	4
	ר	כ	ד	ה	DALET	5
	כ	בּ	ת	כּ	KAF	6
	ת	ר	ב	ד	RESH	7
	כ	ת	ד	ה	CHAF	8

OUR TRADITION — הַבְדָלָה

On Saturday night, after the first three stars can be seen in the sky, שַׁבָּת comes to an end. We have a special ceremony, called הַבְדָלָה, to separate שַׁבָּת from the new week.

הַבְדָלָה means "separation."

In the הַבְדָלָה ceremony we use a cup of wine, a braided candle, and a box filled with sweet spices. We hope that the coming week will be a good one.

What makes a week good?

Write or draw your answer here.

PICTURE PERFECT

Write the word שַׁבָּת below the two objects we can use to welcome שַׁבָּת.

Write the word הַבְדָלָה below the two objects we can use to say goodbye to שַׁבָּת.

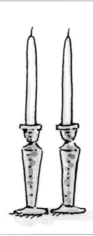

וְאָהַבְתָּ

And You Shall Love

LETTERS YOU KNOW. Say the name and sound of each letter.

בּ ת תּ שׁ מ ל כ ה ר כּ בּ
ד

NEW LETTERS

א ו

VOWELS YOU KNOW. Say the sound of each vowel.

ֱ ְ ָ ַ

ALEF

אַ	אָ	אֱ	אָ	אֱ	אַ 1
בְ	רָ	הֱ	לְ	שָׁ	אָ 2
רְ	כְּ	דָ	אָ	הֱ	אֱ 3

SHAPE IT UP

What does **Alef** look like?
Close your eyes and picture the letter.

Draw it in the air or use your whole body to make the shape of the letter **Alef**.

Make up a clue to remember **Alef**.

HEADS UP!

The letter א is always silent. When it has a vowel under it, we say only the vowel sound.

38

Read lines 1-4 while standing up. Read lines 5-8 while sitting down.

1	אָב	אַתְּ	אַל	אַשׁ	אָד	אָב
2	רָא	שָׁא	אַבָ	אָמְ	אֶדָ	אָבְ
3	בָּא	כָּא	רָא	תָּא	הָא	אָה
4	אַתָּה	אֶדָר	כָּאב	אָהב	אָמַר	אַבָל
5	בָּרָא	רָאה	שָׁאַל	שְׁאָר	אַבָּא	שָׁאַב
6	שָׁאַבְתָּ	רָאֶתָה	אָכְלָה	שְׁאֵלָה	אָמְרה	
7	אָמַרְתְּ	אָכַלְתָּ	מַאֲכָל	בָּרָאתָ	אָכַלְתְּ	
8	אָהַבְתָּ	אֲדָמָה	אַהֲבָה	אֲבְדָה	אַהֲבָה	

I KNOW HEBREW!

Can you find the Hebrew word above?

love = אַהֲבָה

Read it and circle or highlight it.

EXTRA CREDIT

Name the letters in the Hebrew word for *love*.

NAME TAG

Read the name of the Hebrew letter in each box. Circle or highlight its matching Hebrew letter. What sound does the letter make?

ה	ד	(ל)	מ	LAMED	1
ת	ה	ב	ר	HAY	2
כ	ת	ד	ב	VET	3
מ	ל	כ	שׁ	MEM	4
א	ת	ד	ה	ALEF	5
ר	כ	ד	ה	DALET	6
כ	ב	ת	כ	KAF	7
ת	ר	ב	ד	RESH	8

וְ	וַ	וִ	וִ	וַ	וָ	1	**VAV**
הֶ	כְ	רְ	בַּ	דְ	אֲ	2	ו
דְ	רַ	בְּ	בַּ	וַ	וָ	3	

SHAPE IT UP

What does **Vav** look like? Close your eyes and picture the letter.

Draw it in the air or use your whole body to make the shape of the letter **Vav**.

Make up a clue to remember **Vav**.

HEADS UP!

The letter ב and ו make the same sound.

What sound do they make?

Read the odd-numbered lines in a funny voice.
Then read the even-numbered lines with an angry voice.

וְהָ	וְלָ	שֻׁו	תָּו	שָׁו	דָּו	1
וָאְ	וַדְ	וַר	וַת	וָה	וְו	2
בֶּן	תָּו	הָן	כְּ	מָן	לָו	3
אָבָה	לוֹ	אַוֶה	תָּוֶה	שָׁוֶה	דָּו	4
דְּבַשׁ	וָלָד	שָׁוְא	הָוֶה	דָּוֶה	אַתָּר	5
וְאָהַב	וְאַתָּה	רַאֲוֶה	אַדְוָה	אֲשָׁרָה		6
הַדָּבָר	מִלְוָה	וְאָכַל	שַׁלְוָה	אָבְדָה		7
וְאָהַבְתְּ	וְלָמַדְתָּ	וְאָמַרְתָּ	וְאָהַבְתָּ	וְהָלַכְתָּ		8

I KNOW HEBREW!

Can you find this Hebrew word above?

and you shall love = וְאָהַבְתָּ

Read it and circle or highlight it.

EXTRA CREDIT

On what line does וְאָהַבְתָּ appear?

___

41

א

ו

Write the Hebrew word for *love*.

אַהֲבָה

Write the Hebrew word for *and you shall love*.

וְאָהַבְתָּ

How did you do? Circle your best *Alef* and your best *Vav* above.

WORD BUBBLES

With your eyes shut, point to a spot on the page.
Read aloud the word closest to where your finger lands.

Add the number in the circle to your score. Do it three times and see how high you can score.
Play with a partner and see who scores higher.

OUR TRADITION — וְאָהַבְתָּ

וְאָהַבְתָּ means "and you shall love."
The Torah teaches us "to love God with all your heart, and with all your soul,
and with all your might."

We call this teaching the וְאָהַבְתָּ and recite it during services in synagogue.

We also write the וְאָהַבְתָּ on a piece of parchment that is put inside the
mezuzah and hung on the doorposts of our homes.

Why do you think the teaching "love God with all your heart, and with all your soul,
and with all your might" is inside a mezuzah?

SHOW WHAT YOU KNOW

Complete the sentences below using Hebrew words from the word bank.

שַׁבָּת	וְאָהַבְתָּ	בְּרָכָה
שַׁמָּשׁ	הַבְדָּלָה	כַּלָּה

We welcome _____ by saying a _____ over candles.

We use the _____ to light the candles on the Hanukkah menorah.

The special ceremony at the end of Shabbat is called _____.

צְדָקָה
Justice

LETTERS YOU KNOW. Say the name and sound of each letter.

ב כ ר ה כ ל מ שׁ ת ת ב

ד א ו

VOWELS YOU KNOW. Say the sound of each vowel.

קֱ קֱ דָ דָ

NEW LETTERS

צ ק

						KOOF
קֻ	קֱ	קֻ	ק	קֱ	קֻ	1
וּ	כִּ	קֱ	כִּ	רַ	קֻ	2
אֻ	הֵ	כִּ	כַּ	קֱ	קֻ	3

ק

SHAPE IT UP

What does *Koof* look like?
Close your eyes and picture the letter.
Draw it in the air or use your whole body to
make the shape of the letter *Koof*.

Make up a clue to remember *Koof*.

HEADS UP!

The letters ק and כ
make the same sound.

What sound do they make?

44

READY, SET, READ

Read all the words that start with a **Koof**. Then read all the words that end with a **Koof**.
Find and read all the words that don't start or end with a **Koof**.

קַבְּ	וְקָ	קָד	קָב	קָשָׁ	קָרְ	**1**
קָה	קוּ	קָשׁ	קַר	קַל	קָא	**2**
לָק	דַק	אָק	רַק	שַׁק	בַּק	**3**
קָשַׁר	קָדַר	קָשָׁה	קָרָה	קָרָא	קָהָל	**4**
קָרַב	שָׁקַד	קָבַר	קָלָה	קָרְב	מָרָק	**5**
קַבְּלָה	קָשַׁרְתְּ	דַוְקָה	כְּבָרָה	הַרְקָה		**6**
הַבְרָקָה	בְּבַקָשָׁה	בַקָשָׁה	שָׁקַלְתָּ	מַמְתָּק		**7**
בְּבַקָשָׁה	שַׁבָּת	קַבָּלַת	שַׁבָּת	קַבָּלַת		**8**

Great job! 👏

I KNOW HEBREW!

Can you find these Hebrew words above?

Welcoming Shabbat = קַבָּלַת שַׁבָּת

please = בְּבַקָשָׁה

Read then circle or highlight them.

LETTER BOXES

Say the name of the Hebrew letter in each box. Circle or point to the sound each letter makes.

V / **M** / R מ	K / CH / L ק	(H) / V / T ה
T / L / SH ל	V / H / M ו	R / K / D ד

צְ	צַ	צָ	צָ	צָ	צִ	1
לִ	צָ	כְּ	קְ	צַ	קַ	2
דְ	כְּ	קְ	קַ	צָ	צָ	3

TZADEE

צ

SHAPE IT UP

What does *Tzadee* look like?
Close your eyes and picture the letter.

Draw it in the air or use your whole body to make
the shape of the letter *Tzadee*.

Make up a clue to remember *Tzadee*.

HEADS UP!

The letter *Tzadee* makes a
special sound.

Say the words *Matzah Pizza*.

The middle sound in those two
words is the sound
of *Tzadee*.

46

READY, SET, READ

Read lines 1-3 in a strong voice. Read lines 4-6 in a quiet voice. Read lines 7-8 in your regular voice.

צָל	צָה	צָד	צַר	צָב	צַו	1
רָצְ	קָצַ	מָצָ	אָצָ	בָּצַ	כְּצַ	2
צָרָה	אָצָה	בָּצַר	כְּצַד	צָדַק	אָכָה	3
מָצָא	בָּצָל	צְבָת	קָצַר	צָבַּר	צָבָא	4
אָצַר	הַצָּב	מַצָּב	קַצַב	קְצַת	מַצָּה	5
צָמָא	אָצְתְּ	מַצָה	צָמַד	צָלָה	מָצָא	6
צָוְאָה	צַוָּאר	צָרַמְתְּ	וָאָצַר	וְרָצָה	7
צְדָקָה	צָדַקְתְּ	מְצָאתְ	בְּצָרַתְּ	צְדָקָה	8

Which words were extra challenging? Practice reading them with a partner.

I KNOW HEBREW!

Can you find the Hebrew word above?

justice = צְדָקָה

Read it and circle or highlight it.

EXTRA CREDIT

Each year at Passover we eat a special food instead of bread.

Find the name of that food above, then read it aloud. What letter is in the middle of the word?

47

WORD BUBBLES

With your eyes shut, point to a spot on the page.
Read aloud the word closest to where your finger lands.

Add the number in the circle to your score. Do it three times and see how high you can score.
Play with a partner and see who scores higher.

1 שַׁבָּת

2 מַצָּה

3 הַבְּרָכָה

2 וְאָהַבְתָּ

3 קַבָּלַת

1 אַהֲבָה

3 הַבְדָלָה

1 שָׁמֶשׁ

2 צְדָקָה

POWER READING

Read aloud each line without making a mistake. Have a partner time you. How did you do?
Circle or highlight the word that was the most challenging.

מָצָאתָ	צְדָקָה	רְצִתָּה	צָרַמְתָּ	1
אָצַרְתְּ	שְׁאֵלָה	לָבַשְׁתְּ	בְּכִתָּה	2
הַקְּדֻשָׁה	מְלָאכָה	בְּבַקָשָׁה	הַבְדָלָה	3

ק קֻ

צ צ

Write the Hebrew word for **welcoming Shabbat**.

קַבָּלַת שַׁבָּת

Write the Hebrew word for **matzah**.

מַצָּה

Write the Hebrew word for **justice**..

צְדָקָה

How did you do? Circle your best **Koof** and your best **Tzadee** above.

WHAT'S MISSING?

Use the letters above each column to complete the four words in that column.
Read and translate each word.

אָ	רְ	קֻ	דָ		כֻ	שֶׁ	מָ	צָ

5 וְ הַ בָּתְ

6 בְּ כָה

7 צְדָ ה

8 הַבְּ לָה

1 שַׁבָּת

2 לָה

3 מַ ה

4 שֶׁ שׁ

49

OUR TRADITION — צְדָקָה

צְדָקָה means "justice."

When we help other people improve their lives, we make the world more just and fair. The Torah teaches us that it is our responsibility to perform acts of צְדָקָה, acts of justice to help others. One way is to donate money to an organization that helps needy people.

Think of a time when you performed an act of צְדָקָה. Write about it or draw a picture of it here.

WORD MATCH

Match each Hebrew word with its English meaning. Read each Hebrew-English match aloud.

BLESSING	שַׁמָּשׁ
HELPER	בְּרָכָה
JUSTICE	הַבְדָּלָה
BRIDE	שַׁבָּת
SEPARATION	צְדָקָה
SHABBAT	כַּלָה

CHECKPOINT CHALLENGE

Show off your Hebrew reading skills!

Choose a word for a partner to read. Then have your partner choose a word for you to read.
Give yourself one point for every word read correctly. Can you get all 15?

3 דָּבָר	2 בְּרָכָה	1 אַהֲבָה
6 וְאָהַבְתָּ	5 הַבְדָּלָה	4 דְּרָשָׁה
9 לָמַדְתָּ	8 הֲלָכָה	7 כַּלָּה
12 קַבָּלַת	11 צְדָקָה	10 מַצָּה
15 תָּו	14 שַׁבָּת	13 רַבָּה

ALEF BET CHART

You have learned eight new letters in Lessons 4-7:

צ   ק   ו   א   ד   ב   כ   ר

Turn to the **Alef Bet** chart on page 160. Color in the new letters.

How many letters do you now know?
Can you name each letter?

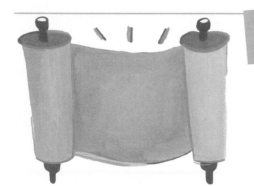

מִצְוָה

Commandment

LETTERS YOU KNOW. Say the name and sound of each letter.

ב כ ר ה כ ל מ שׁ ת ב

ד א ו ק צ

VOWELS YOU KNOW. Say the sound of each vowel.

ֱ ְ ָ ַ

NEW VOWELS

לְ ☐ ☐

.   .

אֲ	וְ	הְ	מְ	תְ	בְּ	1
צְ	לְ	כְּ	רְ	כְ	דְי	2
אְי	בְּי	כְּי	לְי	מְי	וְי	3

לְ ☐ ☐

.   .

Which Hebrew sound reminds you of a buzzing insect?
Circle or highlight it above.

SHAPE IT UP

What does ☐ sound like?

Make a hand motion to show the shape of ☐ as you say its sound.

What does לְ ☐ sound like?

Make a hand motion to show the shape of לְ ☐ as you say its sound.

52

READY, SET, READ

Read lines 1-4. Then, take a break. Stand up and stretch your body. Read lines 5-8.

1	בְּרִי	דָוִ	אֲוִי	לִבִּי	צַדִּי	מִקֵן
2	הֲכִי	צִיר	שְׁמִי	בִּיב	הִכָּה	שִׁשָׁה
3	בְּלִי	בְּכִי	אִמָּא	אִשָׁה	אִישׁ	הִיא
4	תִּיק	דָתִי	בִּימָה	דָוִד	אֲוִיר	רַבִּי
5	קָצִיר	לִבִּיבָה	קְרִיאַת	רִמָּה	תִּירָא	שִׁירָה
6	מִקְרָא	קְהָלָה	אָבִיב	קַדִּישׁ	בְּרִיאַת	צַדִּיק
7	הַתִּקְוָה	תִּקְוָה	מִילָה	בְּרִית	צִיצִית	
8	בַּת מִצְוָה	בַּר מִצְוָה	הַמִּצְוָה	מִצְוָה		

I KNOW HEBREW!

Can you find the Hebrew words above?
Read and circle or highlight them.

knotted fringes on the corners of the tallit = צִיצִית   commandment = מִצְוָה

Kaddish = קַדִּישׁ   bar mitzvah = בַּר מִצְוָה

"The Hope", the national anthem of Israel = הַתִּקְוָה   bat mitzvah = בַּת מִצְוָה

Mommy = אִמָּא

A Hebrew speaker may call their mother אִמָּא.

Write the Hebrew word for "mother." _____

53

Write the Hebrew word for **commandment**.

מִצְוָה מִצְוָה

Write the Hebrew word for **bar mitzvah**.

בַּר מִצְוָה בַּר מִצְוָה

Write the Hebrew word for **bat mitzvah**.

בַּת מִצְוָה בַּת מִצְוָה

Write the Hebrew word for **fringes on the corners of the tallit**.

צִיצִית צִיצִית

Write the Hebrew word for **Kaddish**..

קַדִּישׁ קַדִּישׁ

Write the Hebrew word for **the Hope, the national anthem of Israel**.

הַתִּקְוָה הַתִּקְוָה

RHYME TIME

Read the Hebrew words below.

Connect the rhyming words, then sing them out loud.

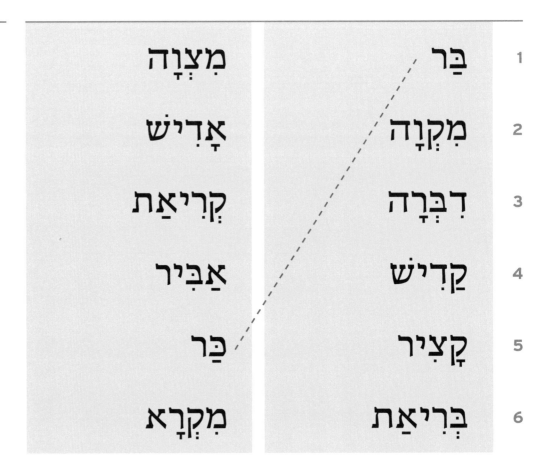

מִצְוָה	בַּר	1
קַדִּישׁ	מִקְוֶה	2
קְרִיאַת	דְּבְרָה	3
אַבִּיר	קַדִּישׁ	4
כַּר	קָצִיר	5
מִקְרָא	בְּרִיאַת	6

OUR TRADITION – מִצְוָה

A מִצְוָה is a commandment from God. These commandments are written in the Torah.

We do a מִצְוָה when we light Shabbat candles, hear the shofar on Rosh Hashanah, honor our parents, feed our pets, or visit a sick friend.

What is a מִצְוָה you have done? Write about it or draw it here.

WORD WIZARD

Read aloud each line. Find the Hebrew letter that is found in every word on the line. Write it on the line.

בּ	דִּבְּרָה	מְדַבָּר	רַבִּי	מַלְבִּיש 1
	מִדְרָשׁ	בְּרִית	בְּקִרְבִּי	אִירָא 2
	אָמַרְתִּי	בִּימָה	מָרָה	תָּמִיד 3
	מִצְוָה	צִיצִית	צְדָקָה	מַצִּיל 4
	בְּשַׁלְוִי	צַוָּה	אָבִיו	הַתִּקְוָה 5
	קְהִילָה	אָהַבְתִּי	אִשָּׁה	לְהָבִיא 6

Write the six letters from these lines below.

					בּ
6	5	4	3	2	1

What does this mean?

55

שְׁמַע

Hear

LETTERS YOU KNOW. Say the name and sound of each letter.

ב כ ר ה כ ל מ שׁ ת ת ב

ד א ו ק צ

VOWELS YOU KNOW. Say the sound of each vowel.

יְ ☐ ☐ ☐ ☐ ☐

NEW LETTER

ע

AYIN

עָ	עִי עְ	עָ	עֵ עֲ	עָ	עַ 1
הֵ	עֲ אֵ	עֶ	הַ	אַ	עַ 2
עֵ	הַ	אֲ הֵ	קִי	צִי	עִי 3

SHAPE IT UP

What does **Ayin** look like?
Close your eyes and picture the letter.

Draw it in the air or use your whole body to make
the shape of the letter **Ayin**.

Make up a clue to remember **Ayin**.

HEADS UP!

The letter ע does not have
its own sound.

When it has a vowel under it,
we say only the vowel sound.

What other letter doesn't have
its own sound?

56

Read line 1 softly, then read line 2 loudly. Continue alternating how you read each line. Then read the lines again, this time reading the odd-numbered lines loudly and the even-numbered lines softly.

1	עָשִׂי	עָתִי	עָב	צָעִי	מַע	דַע
2	עַל	עָבְ	עַד	רַע	עִיר	עַר
3	וַעַד	דַעַת	עַתָּה	רַעַשׁ	בַּעַל	עָבַר
4	שְׁמַע	רָעָב	צָעִיר	תָּקַע	עִמָּה	שָׁעָה
5	רָקִיעַ	עָתִיד	עָשִׁיר	אַרְבַּע	עַתִּיק	עִבְרִי
6	עִבְרִית	מַעֲרִיב	תְּקִיעָה	עֲמִידָה	קְעָרָה	
7	שַׁעֲוָה	עָבַדְתִּי	שִׁבְעָה	עֲתִיקָה	עֲמִידָה	
8	שְׁמַע	תִּשְׁמַע	שְׁמִיעָה	קְרִיאַת	שְׁמַע	

I KNOW HEBREW!

Can you find this Hebrew word above?

hear = שְׁמַע

Read it loudly so that others can **hear** you.

Can you find this Hebrew word above?

Hebrew = עִבְרִית

What letter does it start with?

What letter does it end with?

57

POWER READING

Read aloud each line without making a mistake. Have a partner time you. How did you do? Circle or highlight the word that was the most challenging.

#				
1	צַעַד	לָמַד	שָׁעָה	בַּעַל
2	בָּקַע	עָמַד	שַׁעַר	שָׁעַל
3	בְּרַעַשׁ	בִּשְׁעַת	עֲרִירִי	הִשְׁמִיעַ
4	עֲמִידָה	וְעָצַר	עָבַדְתָּ	עָמְדָה
5	וְדִבַּרְתָּ	וְאָהַבְתָּ	לְהַקְדִּישׁ	אַרְבָּעָה
6	וְעָבַדְתָּ	וְהָאֲדָמָה	וְאָמַרְתָּ	וְאָכַלְתָּ

SOUNDS LIKE

Clap your hands as you read aloud each Hebrew word on the first line.

Circle or highlight the word on each line that sounds the same as the Hebrew in the box. Then compare your answer with a partner's.

#				
1	צַו	עָב	רַב	(צָב)
2	קָרָא	רָקַע	קָרַע	צָבָא
3	אִמָּא	עָמָא	צָמָא	אַתָּה
4	עָשִׁיר	אֲוִיר	עָתִיד	אָשִׁיר
5	מַצָּה	צַעַד	מָצָא	צָמָה
6	דָּבָר	הַדַר	דּוֹר	הָדָד

ע   ע   עְ

Write the Hebrew word for **Hebrew**.

עִבְרִית   עִבְרִית

Write the Hebrew word for **hear**.

שָׁמַע   שָׁמַע

How did you do? Circle your best **Ayin** above.

WORD BUBBLES

With your eyes shut, point to a spot on the page.
Read aloud the word closest to where your finger lands.

Add the number in the circle to your score. Do it three times and see how high you can score.
Play with a partner and see who scores higher.

3	2	1
וְאָהַבְתָּ	שְׁמַע	מַצָּה
2	**3**	**1**
הַתִּקְוָה	עֲמִידָה	צִיצִית
3	**1**	**2**
מַעֲרִיב	תְּקִיעָה	צַדִיק

OUR TRADITION — שְׁמַע

The Hebrew word שְׁמַע means "hear."

שְׁמַע is the first word and the name of one of our most important prayers. The words of שְׁמַע come from the Torah. When we recite the שְׁמַע, we are saying we believe in One God—"Hear O Israel, Adonai is Our God, Adonai is One."

Why do you think we need to tell everyone to hear us? Why can't we just say this in our hearts or to ourselves?

Hand motions can help us think more about the words we say. What hand motions would you do when reciting the שְׁמַע? Write or draw them here.

PICTURE PERFECT

Read each word.

Write the correct word below the matching picture.

צְדָקָה
שְׁמַע
עִבְרִית
כַּלָּה
צִיצִית

נָבִיא

Prophet

LETTERS YOU KNOW. Say the name and sound of each letter.

ב ת ת ש מ ל כ ה ר כ ב

ד א ו ק צ ע

VOWELS YOU KNOW. Say the sound of each vowel.

י ▢ ▢ ▢ ▢ ▢ ▢ ▢
. . ־ֱ ְ ָ ַ

נְ	נָ	נְ	נִ	נְ	נָ	נַ	1
נְ	נִ	עִ	וְ	נִ	רְ	בְ	2
לֵן	דָן	מִין	רָן	מִן	כַּן		3

Which Hebrew sound reminds you of a part of your body?

FINAL NUN/NUN

נ ן

SHAPE IT UP

What do **Nun** and **Final Nun** look like?

Close your eyes and picture the letters.
Draw them in the air or use your whole body to make the shapes of the letters **Nun** and **Final Nun**.

Make up clues to remember **Nun** and **Final Nun**.

HEADS UP!

There are five letters of the Hebrew alphabet that have a different form when they come at the end of a word.

When a נ comes at the end of a word, it is a **Final** ן.

Read lines 1-3 in a happy 🙂 voice. Read lines 4-5 in a sad 🙁 voice.
Read lines 6-8 in your regular voice.

1	נָן	נָו	נְעִי	קַן	בִּין
2	נִין	לָן	דָן	מָן	שִׁין	רָן
3	דִין	בְּנִי	עָנִי	נָקִי	אֲנִי	נָא
4	שָׁנָה	לָבָן	עָנוּ	רְנָה	עָנַד	נַעַר
5	נָבִיא	בִּינָה	נְשָׁמָה	מִשְׁנָה	נְעָרָה
6	מַאֲמִין	שְׁכִינָה	כַּוָּנָה	נְעִילָה	מַרְבִּין
7	רַעֲנָן	מִשְׁכָּן	לְהָבִין	קַנְקַן	לַמְדָן
8	נָבִיא	מְדִינָה	מַה	נִשְׁתַּנָה	נְבִיא

I KNOW HEBREW!

Can you find the Hebrew word above?

prophet = נָבִיא

Read it and circle or highlight it.

EXTRA CREDIT

At the Passover seder, the youngest child asks the Four Questions.

Can you find the two Hebrew words in the lines above that introduce the Four Questions? Read them.

If you remember the tune to the Four Questions, sing the first line!

I SPY

Read aloud each line.

Find the Hebrew that sounds the same as the English in the box. Write the two Hebrew sounds on the line.

עָ	אָ	עֲ	אַ	תַ	צ	הַ	**AH**	1
רְ	הִי	דְיָא	דִי	רִי			**DEE**	2
נָא	בַ	כַ	לָ	וָא			**VAH**	3
כִּי	שִׁי	בְּ	קִי	תִּי			**KEE**	4
אִי	הִיא	תִי	וְי	הִי			**HEE**	5

SOUNDS LIKE

Stomp your foot as you read aloud each line. Which two Hebrew words sound the same? Circle them or show them to a partner.

מָא	מָנָה	מָן	מַה	1
נָוָה	נָע	וְנָא	נָא	2
לְנָוָה	לָוָן	לְבָנָה	לָבָן	3
אֱנָב	עָנָן	אָנָא	עָנוּ	4
עָנָת	עָנִי	אֲנִי	אָנִית	5
קַבָנָא	כַּוָנָה	קָנָה	כִּינַע	6

נ נ נ

ז ן ן

Write the Hebrew word for **prophet**.

נָבִיא נָבִיא

Write the Hebrew word for **Haman**.

הָמָן הָמָן

Do you know who Haman was?

NUN ADD-IN

Complete each word below by adding the correct form of the letter **Nun**.
Then read all the words. When you read the word that means **prophet**, stand up.
When you read the word **Haman**, boo loudly.

3 אֶ ‗ ִ י	2 נָתַ ‗	1 נָ ‗ בִיא
6 ‗ שָ ‗ ֶ ה	5 שָׂמְ ‗ ָ ה	4 הָמָ ‗
9 ‗ לָב	8 כַּן ‗ ֶ ה	7 מַתָ ‗ ָ ה
12 מַה ‗ ִ ישְׁתַ ‗ ָ ה	11 מַאֲמִי ‗	10 מִשְׁכָּ ‗

OUR TRADITION — נָבִיא

The Hebrew word נָבִיא means "prophet."
In the days of the Bible a נָבִיא was a
spokesperson for God. The נָבִיא gave hope
to our people when they felt sad and lost.
These are the names of some of our prophets:
Joshua, Isaiah, Jeremiah, Ezekiel, Hosea,
and Deborah. Our first and greatest
נָבִיא was Moses.

Think about a time when you helped someone
who felt sad or lost. Whom did you help?
What did you say or do? Write about it or draw it here.

WORD POWER

Read aloud the Hebrew words on each line.
Circle or highlight the word that has the same meaning as the English in the box.

קְרִיאַת	כַּוָּנָה	(עִבְרִית)	שָׁנָה	HEBREW	1
נָבִיא	אַרְבַּע	מַעֲרִיב	שְׁכִינָה	PROPHET	2
בְּרִית	וְאָהַבְתָּ	תְּקִיעָה	נְשָׁמָה	AND YOU SHALL LOVE	3
מִצְוָה	אַהֲבָה	אִמָּא	קַדִּישׁ	COMMANDMENT	4
נְעִילָה	מִשְׁכַּן	הַתִּקְוָה	קַבָּלַת	THE HOPE	5

חַלָּה

Braided Bread
for Shabbat and holidays

NEW LETTER

ח

LETTERS YOU KNOW. Say the name and sound of each letter.

ב כ ר ה כ ל מ שׁ ת ת ב

ד א ו ק צ ע נ ן

VOWELS YOU KNOW. Say the sound of each vowel.

יְ

CHET

ח	חָ חֲ	חֲ חִ	חִי	חִ חַ	חַ 1
חָ	כָ חִי	חִי כִי	חַ	כַ 2
הָ	חָ הֲ	הֲ חֲ	הִי	חִ 3

SHAPE IT UP

What does **Chet** look like?
Close your eyes and picture the letter.

Draw it in the air or use your whole body to make the shape of the letter **Chet**.

Make up a clue to remember **Chet**.

HEADS UP!

The letters ח and כ make the same sound.

What sound do these letters make?

66

Read all the words that start with **Chet**, and have a partner read all the words that end with **Chet**. Together read the words that have **Chet** in the middle. Then whisper the words that do not have a **Chet**.

1	חִכְּ	חָבִי	חָתָ	בָּח	אַח	צָח
2	חָל	חִיל	חַד	חָשׁ	חִישׁ	חִימִי
3	קַח	צַח	נָח	לָח	אָח	חַוָּה
4	חִכָּה	שָׁכַח	חָבִיב	חֶבָל	חָתָן	לָקַח
5	חַלָּה	חָלִיל	וְצָחַק	אַחַת	חָצִיר	חָנָן
6	מִנְחָה	חֲמִשָּׁה	שָׁלְחָה	חִירִיק	בָּחַרְתָּ	
7	רַחֲמָן	הָרַחֲמָן	שַׁחֲרִית	חֲתִימָה	חֲדָשָׁה	
8	הַחַלָּה	הַבְּרָכָה	חַלָּה	לְשַׁבָּת	הָרַחֲמָן	

I KNOW HEBREW!

Can you find these Hebrew words above?

the Merciful One (God) = הָרַחֲמָן

braided bread = חַלָּה

Read and circle or highlight them.

EXTRA CREDIT

How many times did you read the word for **braided bread**?

67

LETTER AND VOWEL WORKOUT

You have learned all these letters and vowels!

Say the name of each letter in lines 1-18.

Take turns with a partner reading all the lines. As you do, choose a movement for each line. For example, scratch your head while reading line 1, or rub your hands together while reading line 2.

SOUNDS LIKE

Can you find the Hebrew that sounds like the English word for:

- A hot beverage?
- Something you use to open a lock?
- A buzzing insect?

Circle or highlight those sounds.

אִי	אָ	אֵ	אָ	אַ	1
בִּי	בְּ	בֵּ	בָּ	בֻּ	2
בְי	בְ	בֵ	בָ	בֻ	3
דִי	דְ	דֵ	דָ	דַ	4
הִי	הְ	הֵ	הָ	הַ	5
וְי	וְ	וֵ	וָ	וַ	6
חִי	חְ	חֵ	חָ	חַ	7
כִּי	כְּ	כֵּ	כָּ	כֻּ	8
כִי	כְ	כֵ	כָ	כֻ	9
לִי	לְ	לֵ	לָ	לַ	10
מִי	מְ	מֵ	מָ	מַ	11
נִי	נְ	נֵ	נָ	נַ	12
עִי	עְ	עֵ	עָ	עַ	13
צִי	צְ	צֵ	צָ	צַ	14
קִי	קְ	קֵ	קָ	קַ	15
רִי	רְ	רֵ	רָ	רַ	16
שִׁי	שְׁ	שֵׁ	שָׁ	שַׁ	17
תִי	תְ	תֵ	תָ	תַ	18

68

חַ חַ

Write the Hebrew word for **braided bread**.

חַלָּה

Write the Hebrew word for **Merciful One (God)**.

הָרַחֲמָן

RHYME TIME

Read the words on each line. Three words on each line rhyme. Circle the word that does not rhyme and write it on the line. Now sing aloud the rhyming words.

לָה	אָח	(לָה)	קַח	צַח	1
	כַּלָּה	חָתָן	חָמָה	חַלָּה	2
	מַעֲרִיב	אָבִיב	חָבִיב	אֲבֵדָה	3
	אָשִׁיר	שַׁחֲרִית	עַרְבִית	עִבְרִית	4
	קְרִיאָה	עֲמִידָה	הַנָּבִיא	תְּקִיעָה	5
	שָׁלַח	שָׁכַח	שָׁחַת	לָקַח	6

OUR TRADITION – חַלָה

חַלָה is the braided bread we eat on שַׁבָּת.
When we welcome שַׁבָּת, we recite a בְּרָכָה
over חַלָה, as well as over candles and wine.

Why do you think we eat special bread on Shabbat?

Close your eyes and imagine you're eating חַלָה.
How does it taste? What does it smell like?

EXTRA CREDIT

In a group, recite the בְּרָכָה
we say over candles, wine,
and חַלָה when we
welcome שַׁבָּת.

WORD SKILLS

Read the Hebrew words below. Write the correct Hebrew word above its English meaning.
Read the sentence using the Hebrew word.

בְּרָכָה	חַלָה	שְׁמַע
נָבִיא	צְדָקָה	מִצְוָה

1 We say a _____ to say **Thank You** to God.
   blessing

2 It is a _____ to help feed the hungry.
   mitzvah

3 We eat _____ on שַׁבָּת.
   braided bread

4 A _____ was a spokesperson for God.
   Prophet

5 We say the prayer _____ **O Israel, Adonai is our God, Adonai is One** in the
   morning and evening.   hear

6 When we perform an act of _____ , we are following God's commandments.
   justice

70

עֲלִיָה

Going Up
the honor of being called
up to recite the
blessings over the Torah

NEW LETTER

ל

LETTERS YOU KNOW. Say the name and sound of each letter.

ב כ ר ה כ ל מ שׁ ת ת ב

ד א ו ק צ ע נ ן ח

VOWELS YOU KNOW. Say the sound of each vowel.

ל   ·   ·   -:   :   ָ   ֶ

YUD

לְ ָ	לְ :	לְ ·	לִלְ ·	לְ ָ	לְ _	1

וְלִי	לְלִי ·	וְ :	לְ :	לַ _	לְ _	2

יְדִי	יְדִי	חַי	יְשִׁי	יָן	יָר ָ	יְשָׁ ָ	3

SHAPE IT UP

What does **Yud** look like? Close your eyes and picture the letter.

Draw it in the air or use your whole body to make the shape of the letter **Yud**.

Make up a clue to remember **Yud**.

71

READY, SET, READ

Read aloud the lines below while standing on one foot. Switch to the other foot halfway.

1	יָד	יְהִי	יַיִן	יָמַי	יָדַי	יָמָה
2	שָׁיִשׁ	יָשָׁן	מִיָד	נִיָר	לַיִל	הֲיִי
3	בַּיִת	יָשָׁר	יַעַר	חַיָה	עַיִן	יָשַׁב
4	יָדַע	אַיִל	חַיָב	יָחִיד	יָקָר	מַעְיָן
5	יִצִיר	הָיָה	יָיִן	חַיִל	יָצָא	עֲדַיִן
6	יַחְדוּ	יִרְאָה	יִצְחָק	יַבָּשָׁה	צִיַּרְתִּי	
7	עֲלִיָה	כְּוִיָה	יוֹכַח	יַלְדָה	יְדִיעָה	
8	יְשִׁיבָה	יִשְׁתַּבַּח	הָיְתָה	מִנְיָן	עֲלִיָה	

I KNOW HEBREW!

Can you find these Hebrew words above?

aliyah, going up = עֲלִיָה

minyan, ten Jewish adults, the minimum needed to recite some prayers = מִנְיָן

Read and circle or highlight them.

EXTRA CREDIT

Can you find the word יָד above? It is the Hebrew word for **hand**.

It is also the word for the pointer used to touch the parchment of the Torah.

יָ וָ וְ

Write the Hebrew word for **aliyah, going up**.

עֲלִיָּה עֲלִיָּה

Write the Hebrew word for **minyan, ten Jewish adults**.

מִנְיָן מִנְיָן

YUD DETECTIVE

Each word to the right contains at least one **Yud**.

With a partner, take turns reading all the words that begin with **Yud**. When your partner reads a word correctly, raise your יָד, your hand. Cross out or circle all the words read correctly.

Yud is the smallest letter in the Hebrew alphabet. Read in a small voice all the words that are left.

יְמָמָה	תְּחִיָּה	שִׁירָה	יַדְעָן	1
יִצְחָק	יַלְדָּה	יַעֲנָה	עֲנִיבָה	2
מַכִּיר	קְנִיָּה	יָקָר	יָנַק	3
בַּיִת	שִׁירָה	בְּנִי	הִיא	4
נָדִיר	קַמְתִּי	יַחַד	רִיב	5
נָבִיא	עֲנִיבָה	חָבִיב	יְקָרָה	6
אַיִן	יַבָּשָׁה	יָצַב	יְדִיעָה	7
יָהִיר	עִנְיָן	יָשַׁבְתָּ	יֵשַׁע	8
רְצִינִי	יָרַשְׁתָּ	יָמִין	עַיִן	9

EXTRA CREDIT

Circle any word that has a silent yud that is part of the vowel EE (יִ)

Write that word. _____

73

OUR TRADITION – עֲלִיָּה

In the synagogue, the honor of being called up to the Torah is known as an עֲלִיָּה.
The word עֲלִיָּה means "going up." We go up to the *bimah* and recite blessings before
and after each section of the Torah is read.

The word עֲלִיָּה also has another meaning. If someone moves to Israel, that person
is making עֲלִיָּה, because they are going up to the land of Israel, the Holy Land.

Have you ever seen someone being called up for an עֲלִיָּה?
Did the person look nervous, proud, excited, or something else? How would you feel?

CONNECTIONS

Read the word parts in each column.

Connect the beginning of a word in the right column to its ending in the left column.

Read each word aloud.

וָה	שַׁ	1
הַבְּתָ	הַבְ	2
יָן	בְּרְ	3
דָלָה	וְאָ	4
בָּת	צָדְ	5
יָה	מְצְ	6
קָה	מִנְ	7
כָה	עַל	8

74

לְחַיִּים

To Life

NEW LETTER

ם

LETTERS YOU KNOW. Say the name and sound of each letter.

ב ת ת שׁ מ ל כ ה ה ר כ ב

ד א ו ק צ ע נ ן ח י

VOWELS YOU KNOW. Say the sound of each vowel.

י ❑ ❑ ❑ ❑ ❑ ❑

. ֵ ֱ ְ ָ ַ

FINAL MEM

ם

חַם	אִם	דָם	צָם	קָם	תָּם		**1**
עִם	רָם	בָּם	יָם	שָׁם	עַם		**2**
אִים	הָם	לִים	רַיִם	תִּים	יִים		**3**

SHAPE IT UP

What does *Final Mem* look like?
Close your eyes and picture the letter.
Draw it in the air or use your whole body
to make the shape of the letter
Final Mem.

Make up a clue to remember
Final Mem.

HEADS UP!

There are five letters in the Hebrew alphabet that have a
different form when they come at the end of a word.

When a מ comes at the end of a word, it is a *Final* ם.

What other letter have you learned that has a different form
at the end of a word?

Write that letter here: _____.

Write that letter in its final form here: _____.

Read aloud each line. When you read a word that ends in the sound "eem," stand up.
When you read a word that ends in "ahm," sit down.

1	הָלַם	אַחִים	עָלִים	מִרְיָם	בַּדִּים	תְּרַם
2	אִיִּם	שְׁנַיִם	בָּתִּים	אָדָם	דַּקִּים	מִצְרַיִם
3	חָכָם	רַעַם	יָמִים	רַבִּים	חַיִּים	דָּמַם
4	בָּנִים	מַיִם	אָדָם	שְׁתַּיִם	מִלִּים	אָשָׁם
5	נָשִׁים	שָׁמַיִם	דְּבָרִים	יָדַיִם	קָמִים	עָלִים
6	אַבְרָהָם	נְבִיאִים	כְּרָמִים	שִׁבְעִים	אֲנָשִׁים	
7	עִבְרִים	רַחֲמִים	יְלָדִים	צַדִּיקִים	מְלָכִים	
8	עֲבָדִים	יְצִיאַת	מִצְרַיִם	לְחַיִּים	לְחַיִּים	

I KNOW HEBREW!

Can you find these Hebrew words above?

to life = לְחַיִּים
the name of the first human in the Torah = אָדָם
the Exodus, going out from Egypt = יְצִיאַת מִצְרַיִם

Read and circle or highlight them.

WORD BUBBLES

With your eyes shut, point to a spot on the page. Read the word closest to where your finger lands.

Add the number in the circle to your score. Do it three times and see how high you can score.
Play with a partner and see who scores higher.

Want a higher score? Earn one point for each word translated correctly.

VOCABULARY CHALLENGE

You know the English meaning of many of the words in the **Word Bubbles** activity above.
Read the Hebrew and give the English meaning for the words you know.

מַ מַ ⃗מַ

Write the Hebrew word for **the first human in the Torah**.

אָדָם אָדָם

Write the Hebrew word for **To Life!**

לְחַיִים לְחַיִים

Write the Hebrew words for **Exodus from Egypt**.

יְצִיאַת מִצְרַיִם יְצִיאַת מִצְרַיִם

HEADS UP!

מ and ם have the same sound. How are they different?

Make up a clue to help you remember the difference between מ and ם.

_____

Complete each word by adding the correct form of **Mem**.

Read the words to a partner. Do you know the meanings of some of the words?

How many?_____

3 ע __ שׁ	2 ן __ הָ	1 שְׁנַ__ים
6 בְּרְכַּ__י	5 __אַבְרָקָה	4 הָרַחַ__ן
9 __צָוֶה	8 יָמֵי__	7 לְחַיִי__
12 __צָרַיִם	11 אָדָ__	10 __נִין

OUR TRADITION — לְחַיִּים

לְחַיִּים means "to life." At a special celebration, such as a wedding or graduation, it is traditional to clink our glasses together and say לְחַיִּים!

The word חַיִּים means "life" and appears in many of our prayers.

When would you say לְחַיִּים? Write about it or draw it here.

WORD POWER

Read aloud the Hebrew words on each line.
Circle or highlight the word that has the same meaning as the English in the box.

שָׁמָשׁ	הַבְדָלָה	חַלָּה	(בְּרָכָה)	BLESSING	1
לַחַיִּים	עֲבָדִים	חָכָם	מִצְוָה	TO LIFE	2
שְׁתַּיִם	שָׁמַע	בָּנִים	נָבִיא	HEAR	3
יְצִיאַת	עַיִן	עֲלִיָּה	מִצְרַיִם	GOING UP	4
יְשִׁיבָה	צְדָקָה	שָׁמַיִם	יְלָדִים	JUSTICE	5

79

CHECKPOINT CHALLENGE

Show off your Hebrew reading skills! Choose a word for your partner to read.
Then have your partner choose a word for you to read. Give yourself one point for every word read correctly. Continue until you have read all the words.

4 צַדִּיק	3 נָבִיא	2 רַבִּי	1 אִמָּא
8 לַחַיִּים	7 אָחִי	6 דָּוִד	5 יְהִי
12 מִצְוָה	11 עֲלִיָּה	10 לְכִי	9 כִּי
16 צִיצִית	15 עִבְרִית	14 נִין	13 אֲנִי
20 הַתִּקְוָה	19 שִׁירָה	18 בְּרִית	17 תְּקִיעָה

Which box contains the boy's name David? _____

ALEF BET CHART

You have learned six new letters in Lessons 9-13:

ם   י   ח   ן נ   ע

Turn to the **Alef Bet** chart on page 160. Color in the new letters.
Can you say the name and sound of each letter you now know?

LESSON 14

תּוֹרָה

Torah, Teaching

NEW VOWELS

וֹ

LETTERS YOU KNOW. Say the name and sound of each letter.

ב כ ר ה כ ל מ שׁ ת ב

ם מ י ח נ ע צ ק ו א ד

VOWELS YOU KNOW. Say the sound of each vowel.

י ‧ ‧ ֽ: ֽ ָ ‧

וֹ

נוֹ	דוֹ	לוֹ	מוֹ	רוֹ	בוֹ	תוֹ		1
יֹ	חֹ	נֹ	עֹ	קֹ	צֹ	אֹ		2
דוֹשׁ	קֹב	שׁוֹן	אָנֹ	עוֹת	מֹעַ			3

SHAPE IT UP

What does וֹ sound like? Make a hand motion to show the shape of וֹ as you say its sound.

What does ‧ sound like? Make a hand motion to show the shape of ‧ as you say its sound.

Look at lines 1-3 above. What sounds like:

The opposite of "yes"? Write it in Hebrew here: _____

The opposite of "high"? Write it in Hebrew here: _____

HEADS UP!

Usually a vowel is found below a letter: שַׁ ‏רְ.

But the vowel וֹ or ‧ comes after a letter:

מ וֹ ת.

81

READY, SET, READ

Read aloud the odd-numbered lines. Read aloud the even-numbered lines.

צֹאן	חוֹל	יוֹם	אוֹת	לֹא	כֹּל	1
חוֹר	צוֹם	שׁוֹר	מוֹת	קוֹל	עוֹד	2
כְּמוֹ	אָנֹכִי	דָתוֹ	אַתֶּם	יָבֹא	שָׁמַע	3
שָׁעוֹת	נָכוֹן	לָשׁוֹן	כָּבוֹד	מְאֹד	אָבוֹת	4
מְלֹא	תְּהֹם	מוֹרָה	צִיּוֹן	תּוֹרָה	קָדוֹשׁ	5
עוֹלָם	אָדוֹן	יַעֲקֹב	אַהֲרֹן	שְׁלֹמֹה		6
הַשָּׁנָה	רֹאשׁ	שָׁלוֹם	שַׁבָּת	הַמּוֹצִיא		7
כֹּהֲנִים	דוֹרוֹת	מִצְווֹת	בְּרָכוֹת	תּוֹרָה		8

How did you do? Choose four words that were challenging to read. Read them again to a partner.

I KNOW HEBREW!

Can you find these Hebrew words above?
Circle or point to them. Then read each word.

Torah, teaching =
תּוֹרָה

Holy =
קָדוֹשׁ

Hello, goodbye, peace =
שָׁלוֹם

A peaceful Shabbat =
שַׁבָּת שָׁלוֹם

Blessing over bread =
הַמּוֹצִיא

Jewish New Year =
רֹאשׁ הַשָּׁנָה

EXTRA CREDIT

Can you find the name of the **Jewish New Year** in the words above?

Write it here._____

Can you recite the בְּרָכָה
we say over חַלָה?

WORD BUBBLES

With your eyes shut, point to a spot on the page. Read the word closest to where your finger lands.

Add the number in the circle to your score. Do it three times and see how high you can score.
Play with a partner and see who scores higher.

Want a higher score? Earn one point for each word translated correctly.

1
עֲלִיָּה

2
מִנְיָן

3
עוֹלָם

2
נְשָׁמָה

1
שָׁלוֹם

3
כַּוָּנָה

1
בְּרִית

2
תּוֹרָה

3
שַׁחֲרִית

1
שְׁמַע

WORD RIDDLE

My name means "peace." It also means "hello" and "goodbye."

My name contains the vowel וֹ.

Who am I?

Write the Hebrew words for **a peaceful Shabbat**.

שַׁבָּת שָׁלוֹם

Write the Hebrew word for the **blessing over bread**.

הַמּוֹצִיא

Write the Hebrew words for the **Jewish New Year**.

רֹאשׁ הַשָּׁנָה

Write the Hebrew word for **Torah**.

תּוֹרָה

Write the Hebrew word for **holy**.

קָדוֹשׁ

Write the Hebrew word for **hello**, **goodbye**, and **peace**.

שָׁלוֹם

RHYME TIME

Read the words on each line and find the three that rhyme. Then, sing the rhyming words aloud.

בַּת	הַר	קַר	בַּר	1
תּוֹר	חוֹר	חוֹם	שׁוֹר	2
מוֹרָה	אוֹרָה	לִקְרֹא	תּוֹרָה	3
נָכוֹן	עוֹלָם	שָׁעוֹן	לָשׁוֹן	4
רוֹצָה	שָׁלוֹשׁ	רֹאשׁ	קָדוֹשׁ	5
הַכֹּל	קוֹל	חוֹל	דוֹר	6
בְּרִיוֹת	שָׁנוֹת	חַיּוֹת	אוֹתוֹ	7
חֲלוֹם	חַלוֹת	אָדוֹם	שָׁלוֹם	8

EXTRA CREDIT

The Hebrew word for the number three starts and ends with the same letter, שׁ.

Can you find it above?

Read all the words on that line.

WORD RIDDLE

I am a word repeated three times in a row when we recite the עֲמִידָה. I mean "holy." I begin with the letter ק. Who am I?

84

OUR TRADITION — תּוֹרָה

The word תּוֹרָה means "teaching" and is the name of the Five Books of Moses. The תּוֹרָה teaches us how to live good and compassionate lives. The stories in the תּוֹרָה tell us about our ancestors Abraham and Sarah, Isaac and Rebecca, and Jacob, Leah, and Rachel. We read portions of the תּוֹרָה each week in the synagogue to help us remember its ideas and lessons.

Why do you think we reread the same words of the Torah year after year?

Why might it be helpful to read stories of our ancestors who lived thousands of years ago?

CONNECTIONS

Read the word in each column.

Connect each word in column א with a word in column ב to make a phrase.

Say the phrase out loud.

ב	א
נִשְׁתַּנָה	שַׁבָּת
מִצְוָה	מַה
שָׁלוֹם	רֹאשׁ
הַשָּׁנָה	יְצִיאַת
מִצְרַיִם	בַּת

85

טַלִּית

Tallit,
Prayer Shawl

NEW LETTER
ט

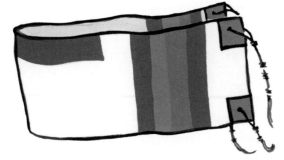

LETTERS YOU KNOW. Say the name and sound of each letter.

ב כ ר ה כ ל מ שׁ ת ת ב

ד א ו ק צ ע נ ן ח י ם

VOWELS YOU KNOW. Say the sound of each vowel.

וֹ יִ   ִ   ֵ   ֱ   ָ   ַ

ִ

TET

ט

ט	טִי	טוֹ	טִ	טֵ	טַ	1
מִ	טִ	מָ	טָ	מוֹ	טוֹ	2
נְטִי	טָר	בָּט	עַט	בָּט	טָשׁ	טָה	3

SHAPE IT UP

What does *Tet* look like?

Close your eyes and picture the letter.

Draw it in the air or use your whole body to make
the shape of the letter *Tet*.

Make up a clue to remember *Tet*.

READY, SET, READ

Read aloud all the words that begin with **Tet**. Find all the words that end with **Tet** and read those too.
Then read all the words that neither start nor end with **Tet**.

1	טוֹן	טִיב	מָט	אַט	חַיְט	מוֹטוֹ
2	טוֹב	טַל	אִטִי	טָרִי	שׁוֹט	קָט
3	מִטָה	מוֹט	קָטָן	חִטָה	שָׁחַט	לָטַשׁ
4	לְאַט	מָטָר	חָטָא	מְעַט	שִׁבָט	בָּטַח
5	טַלִית	טָהוֹר	אָטָד	טַעַם	טִבְעִי	טָמַן
6	קְטַנָה	עֲטָרָה	מִקְלָט	חֲטָאִים	הַבִּיטָה
7	שְׁבָטִים	טוֹבִים	בִּטָחוֹן	נְטִילַת	יָדַיִם
8	טַלִית	שָׁנָה	טוֹבָה	יוֹם	טוֹב

Great job!

I KNOW HEBREW!

Can you find these words above?

טַלִית = *tallit, prayer shawl*

יוֹם טוֹב = *holiday, festival*

שָׁנָה טוֹבָה = *Happy New Year*

On what Jewish holiday would you say שָׁנָה טוֹבָה?
Read and circle or highlight them.

87

SOUNDS LIKE

Read aloud each line.

Circle or highlight the Hebrew sounds on each line that are the same.

1	כָּתְיָה	עַתָּה	הָאַתְּ	אַתָּה
2	תָּאַר	תּוֹתָח	טָאַר	מוֹתָה
3	כָּלַת	קָלָה	כָּלָה	לָקַח
4	מָחָר	חָמָת	כַּמָה	מָכַר
5	עָנָב	בָעָע	עָנוּ	וַנָּו
6	לִתָת	נָתָה	לְאַט	נָטַע
7	שְׁלִיטָה	כְּלִית	קְלִיטָה	שְׁתִיָה
8	כּוֹרָה	רַכַּת	דַכוֹת	דַקוֹת

(עַתָּה and אַתָּה circled in line 1)

HEADS UP!

The letters ט, ת, and תּ make the same sound. What sound do they make?

WORD WIZARD

A phrase you know is hidden below! Cross out the Hebrew letters and their vowels that match the English sounds below. Write the remaining Hebrew letters with their vowels.

1	CHAH
2	YEE

3	MOH
4	LAH

5	N
6	EE

ן	ה	כָּ	בָ	מוֹ	טוֹ		ה	לָ	נָ	יִי	שָׁ	עִי

טוֹ

What does the phrase mean? _____

ט טֹ ט

Write the Hebrew word for **tallit, prayer shawl**.

טַלִּית טַלִית

Write the Hebrew words for **Happy New Year**.

שָׁנָה טוֹבָה שָׁנָה טוֹבָה

Write the Hebrew words for **holiday, festival**.

יוֹם טוֹב יוֹם טוֹב

I SPY

Find the Hebrew that sounds the same as the English in the box. Write the two Hebrew sounds on the line or read them to a partner.

הַ הֶ		הֵ	תָ	הַ	חָ	חֵ	HA	1
צִי	עִי	אַ	צִ	אִי			EE	2
נֹ	כֹ	ו	נוֹ	ווֹ			NO	3
תָ	כַ	הֵ	חַ	ח			CHAH	4
לֹ	וְיא	לִי	יֹ	וְי			VEE	5
טָ	מַ	אֵ	טַ				TAH	6
נ	ד	ן	ר	ו			N	7
ווֹ	י	בֹ	כֹ	רוֹ			VO	8
חִי	כִּי	לֹ	בִּי	קִי			KEE	9
ח	מ	ה	ם	ן			M	10
צַ	עֵ	צָ	עַ				TSAH	11
וֹ	רֹ	תֹ	דוֹ	רוֹ			RO	12

OUR TRADITION — טַלִּית

טַלִּית is the Hebrew word for "prayer shawl."
Many Jewish adults wear a טַלִּית during
morning prayer services. The four corners of
the טַלִּית have knotted fringes called צִיצִית.
The תּוֹרָה tells us to look at the צִיצִית so
that we will remember to follow God's commandments.

You might choose to wear a טַלִּית when you are
a Jewish adult.

Draw a picture of yourself wearing a טַלִּית.
Or, draw a picture of an adult you know
wearing a טַלִּית.

SHOW WHAT YOU KNOW

Connect each Hebrew word with its English meaning.

BLESSING	צְדָקָה	TORAH	הַבְדָּלָה
PRAYER SHAWL	שַׁבָּת	GOING UP	בַּת
JUSTICE	בְּרָכָה	SEPARATION	תּוֹרָה
SHABBAT	טַלִּית	DAUGHTER	עֲלִיָּה

HOLY	שְׁמַע	PROPHET	מִצְוָה
TO LIFE	וְאָהַבְתָּ	BRAIDED BREAD	שַׁמָּשׁ
HEAR	לְחַיִּים	HELPER	נָבִיא
AND YOU SHALL LOVE	קָדוֹשׁ	COMMANDMENT	חַלָּה

CHECKPOINT CHALLENGE

Show off your Hebrew reading skills!

Read aloud each word. Give yourself one point for every word read correctly.

1 אוֹת	2 רִבּוֹנוּ	3 כְּבוֹד	4 קָדוֹשׁ
5 טָהוֹר	6 מִצְוֹת	7 חוֹל	8 טוֹב
9 צִיּוֹן	10 כֹּהֲנִים	11 נָכוֹן	12 שָׁלוֹם
13 הַמּוֹצִיא	14 נוֹרָא	15 עוֹלָם	16 צוֹם
17 קוֹל	18 רֹאשׁ	19 לָשׁוֹן	20 תּוֹרָה

Earn another point for each word you can translate into English.

How did you do?

אֱמֶת

Truth

NEW VOWELS

ֵ   ֶ

LETTERS YOU KNOW. Say the name and sound of each letter.

ב כ ר ה כ ל מ שׁ ת ת ב

ם ח י נ ע ק צ א ו ד

ט

VOWELS YOU KNOW. Say the sound of each vowel.

וֹ   י   ִ   ֵ   ְ   ָ   ַ

ִ

יֵ	אֶ	טֵ	תֶ	בֶּ	דֶ		1
צֶ	קֶ	לֶ	מֶ	עֶ	שֶׁ		2
יֵה	דֵשׁ	חֵלִי	רֵב	עֵד	תֵּם		3

SHAPE IT UP

What does ֶ sound like? Make a hand motion to show the shape of ֶ as you say its sound.

What does ֵ sound like? Make a hand motion to show the shape of ֵ as you say its sound.

92

Choose two lines for a partner to read aloud. Then have your partner choose two lines for you to read. Continue until you've each read every line on the page.

1	אֶת	אֶל	שֶׁלִּי	שֶׁלֹּא	אֱמֶת	אַתֶּן
2	אֲשֶׁר	שֶׁמֶשׁ	יֶלֶד	לָכֶם	אֹהֶל	אֶבֶן
3	אַתֶּם	נֶצַח	חֹדֶשׁ	כֹּתֶל	טֶרֶם	אֶחָד
4	רוֹצֶה	שֶׁבַע	עֶרֶב	מוֹרֶה	נֶאֱמָן	שְׁמוֹנֶה
5	וְנֶאֱמַר	מְחַיֶּה	רוֹעֶה	עוֹלֶה	הֶחָלִיט	יִהְיֶה
6	לְעוֹלָם	וָעֶד	תּוֹרַת	אֱמֶת	מִצְוָה	אֶתְכֶם
7	אֲרוֹן	הַקֹּדֶשׁ	כֶּתֶר	וַיֹּאמֶר	תּוֹרָה	אֱלֹהִים
8	אֱלֹהִים	הַמּוֹצִיא	לֶחֶם	אֱמֶת	וְצֶדֶק	

I KNOW HEBREW!

Can you find these Hebrew words above?

truth = אֱמֶת

God = אֱלֹהִים

Who brings forth bread = הַמּוֹצִיא לֶחֶם

the Holy Ark = אֲרוֹן הַקֹּדֶשׁ

Read and circle or highlight them.

EXTRA CREDIT

What is the first letter in the Hebrew word for truth? ___

How many other words above start with that letter? ___

PRAYER PRACTICE

All the words to the right are found in prayers or blessings. Practice reading them aloud.

The word לֶחֶם means bread. We say a blessing over bread on Shabbat. What is the name of the braided bread we eat on Shabbat? Write it here:

_____

The word אֶחָד means one. We say an important prayer about our belief in one God. Can you remember the name of that prayer?

(Hint: the name of the prayer starts with a **Shin**.)

Write its name in Hebrew here:_____

1 הַמוֹצִיא לֶחֶם

2 וַיֹּאמֶר מֹשֶׁה

3 לְעוֹלָם וָעֶד

4 אֲדֹנָי אֶחָד

5 מִי כָמֹכָה נֶאְדָּר בַּקֹּדֶשׁ

6 אֱלֹהִים בָּרָא אֶת הַשָּׁמַיִם

7 אֲשֶׁר אָנֹכִי מְצַוֶּה אֶתְכֶם

8 כִּי עֶבֶד נֶאֱמָן קָרָאתָ לּוֹ

HEADS UP!

Sometimes, the dot on the letter שׁ has to do two jobs. You can call it the double-duty dot.

מֹשֶׁה = מֹ שֶׁה

Can you explain what two jobs the dot has to do in these words?

קָדֹשׁ רֹשֶׁם שָׁלֹשׁ עֲשֶׂר מֹשֶׁה

I SPY

Find the Hebrew word on each line that sounds the same as the English in the box.
Write the Hebrew word on the line or read it to a partner.

1	ALIYAH	צִיּוֹן	(עֲלִיָּה)	הֲלָכָה	עֲלִיָּה
2	TALLIT	מִנְיָן	טוֹבָה	טַלִּית	
3	SHALOM	עוֹלָם	אָרוֹן	שָׁלוֹם	
4	MATZAH	הַמּוֹצִיא	מַצָּה	מִנְחָה	
5	AMIDAH	תְּקִיעָה	נְשָׁמָה	עֲמִידָה	
6	KADDISH	צַדִּיק	קַדִּישׁ	בְּרִית	
7	SHEMA	שְׁמַע	שֶׁמֶשׁ	שַׁבָּת	

Describe what שָׁלוֹם means to you.

WRITING PRACTICE

Write the Hebrew word for **truth**.

אֱמֶת

Write the Hebrew word for **God**.

אֱלֹהִים

Write the Hebrew words for the **Holy Ark**.

אֲרוֹן הַקֹּדֶשׁ

Write the Hebrew words for **Who brings forth bread**.

הַמּוֹצִיא לֶחֶם

OUR TRADITION – אֱמֶת

The Hebrew word אֱמֶת means "truth."

In our prayers we say that God's words are true and righteous: אֱמֶת וְצֶדֶק.

The Ten Commandments instruct us to tell the truth—אֱמֶת.

Relationships between people must be built on אֱמֶת, on trust and truth.

Why is it important to tell the truth—אֱמֶת—to our family and friends?

SHOW WHO YOU KNOW

Match each Hebrew name with its translation. Read each match aloud.
Do you know anyone with those names?

MIRIAM	חַנָּה	MOSES	אָדָם
REBECCA	דְּבוֹרָה	BENJAMIN	מֹשֶׁה
HANNAH	רִבְקָה	ADAM	דָּוִד
DEBORAH	מִרְיָם	DAVID	בִּנְיָמִן

פֶּסַח

Passover
the feast of
unleavened bread

LETTERS YOU KNOW. Say the name and sound of each letter.

ב כ ר ה ה מ ל כ ש ת ת ב

ם י ח נ ע צ ק ו א ד

ט

VOWELS YOU KNOW. Say the sound of each vowel.

וֹ יִ ָ ַ ֵ ֶ ְ ֶ ֵ

ֱ ֳ

ִ

PAY

פ

פָ	פ	פִ	פַ	פֶ	פֶ	פוֹ	1
פְּתִי	פַת	פַת	פֶן	פֹה	פְּרִי	פֶה	2
פְּרֶ	פְּרֶ	טפֹ	כַפִּי	צְפוֹ	פֶּשַ	פְּשָ	3

Which word above sounds like something you write with? Write it in Hebrew here:_____

SHAPE IT UP

What does **Pay** look like? Close your eyes and picture the letter.
Draw it in the air or use your whole body to make the shape of the letter **Pay**.

Make up a clue to remember **Pay**.

READY, SET, READ

Remember that the letter **Pay** makes the sound of the English letter **P**.
Read aloud lines 1-3 like you're **p**owerful. Read lines 4-6 in a **p**olite voice.
Read lines 7-8 with a **p**ause between each sound.

1	אַפּוֹ	פִּיל	פָּנָה	פַּחַד	מִפִּי	פֶּרַח
2	טִפָּה	כַּפַּיִם	צִפּוֹר	פָּתַח	דַּפִּים	כַּפִּית
3	פְּשָׁט	פַּעַם	פֶּלֶא	פֶּשַׁע	פֶּרֶק	כִּפָּה
4	פּוֹדֶה	מַפָּה	פָּקַד	פָּחוֹת	יִפֹּל	תָּפֵל
5	פִּדְיוֹן	פַּרְצִי	פְּלוֹנִי	יִשְׁפָּט	מִשְׁפָּט	פַּרְעֹה
6	פָּרָשָׁה	כַּפָּרָה	מַשְׁפִּיעַ	צִפּוֹרָה	עִפָּרוֹן	
7	פְּעָמִים	פָּתַחְתָּ	אַלְפַּיִם	הַשְׁפָּעָה	פִּתְאֹם	
8	מִשְׁפָּחָה	מִשְׁפָּטִים	מִתְפַּלְלִים	פְּרָחִים		

Great job!

Now read any four words **p**erfectly. Give yourself a **p**at on the back!

I KNOW HEBREW!

Can you find these Hebrew words above?

family = מִשְׁפָּחָה

kippah, skullcap = כִּפָּה

pencil = עִפָּרוֹן

Read and circle or highlight them.

EXTRA CREDIT

Can you find the Hebrew word for **Pharaoh**
in the lines above? (Hint: it's on line 5.)

What do you know about **Pharaoh**?

98

RHYME TIME

Read aloud the words to the right. Find the two rhyming words on each line. Circle them or read them to a partner.

1	נוֹרָא	צוֹם	תּוֹרָה	אוֹת	
2	יוֹרָם	מוֹצִיא	הוֹצִיא	הוֹלְכִים	
3	תֶּרֶק	לֶחֶם	כֶּתֶר	רֶחֶם	
4	פֶּרֶק	טִפָּה	פֶּרַח	כִּפָּה	
5	טָהוֹר	טַלִּית	מִטָּה	שָׁחוֹר	
6	פִּדְיוֹן	פְּעָמִים	פִּתְאֹם	עִפָּרוֹן	

SAMECH

1	סַ	סְ	סִי	סוֹ	סֻ	ס	סֶ
2	סַל	סַע	סֶלָה	סָב	סַם	סִיר	
3	חַס	יְסוֹ	סִין	סַב	מְס	נַס	

SHAPE IT UP

What does **Samech** look like?

Close your eyes and picture the letter.

Draw it in the air or use your whole body to make the shape of the letter **Samech**.

Make up a clue to remember **Samech**.

99

READY, SET, READ

Read aloud the first word on every line. Next, read the second word on every line.
Then take a minute to stretch or walk around the room. Now you're ready to read more!
Practice reading aloud the words you haven't read yet.

1	כּוֹס	סֶלַע	מַס	פֶּסַח	סְתָו	סִיָן
2	סְתָם	חֶסֶד	סַבָּא	סָבְתָא	חָסִיד	כַּסְפּוֹ
3	נִיסָן	סִדְרָה	חַסְדוֹ	סַנְדָק	יְסוֹד	מִסְפָּר
4	מָסֹרֶת	נִסִּים	נִכְנָס	כְּסוֹד	מְנַסֶּה	לַעֲסֹק
5	סְבִיבוֹן	מִסָבִיב	בָּסִיס	הִסְפִּיד	וְנִסְכּוּ	מַחְסִי
6	מִסְפֶּרֶת	כְּנֶסֶת	הַכְּנֶסַת	נִסְפַּח	מַסְפִּיק	
7	חֲסָדִים	חֲסִידִים	פַּרְנָסָה	סְלִיחָה	סְלִיחוֹת	
8	פֶּסַח	כַּרְפַּס	חֲרֹסֶת	מַצָּה	מָרוֹר	פֶּסַח

Were any words especially challenging to read? Practice reading those again.

HOLIDAY CHALLENGE

Read all the words on line 8 above. All the words on line 8 are from a holiday.
Write the name of that holiday in English here:

_____

How many of those are words for things you can eat?

_____

פ

ס

Write the Hebrew word for **Passover**.

פֶּסַח

Write the Hebrew word for **kindness**.

חֶסֶד

Write the Hebrew word for **kippah, skullcap**.

כִּפָּה

Write the Hebrew word for **family**.

מִשְׁפָּחָה

WORD BUBBLES

With your eyes shut, point to a spot on the page. Read the word closest to where your finger lands.

Add the number in the circle to your score. Do it three times and see how high you can score. Play with a partner and see who scores higher.

Want a higher score? Earn one point for each word translated correctly.

OUR TRADITION — פֶּסַח

When our people were slaves in Egypt, God sent מֹשֶׁה to lead us out of Egypt to freedom. We celebrate this event each spring with the festival of פֶּסַח. Every year we retell the פֶּסַח story when we read the haggadah.

Draw a picture or write about how you celebrate the festival of פֶּסַח. What is your favorite part of פֶּסַח?

THE פֶּסַח SEDER

Read aloud each Hebrew word and its English meaning. Read each sentence describing a פֶּסַח food. What is the correct Hebrew word to each question?

מָרוֹר	מַצָּה	חֲרוֹסֶת	כַּרְפַּס	יַיִן
bitter herbs	matzah	chopped apples and nuts, *charoset*	greens	wine

1 Everyone was in a hurry to leave Egypt and did not have time to wait for the bread dough to rise. My dough hardened into a flat, crunchy kind of bread.

Who am I? _____

2 I am the greens on the seder plate. I represent springtime and new life. I am dipped into salt water to remind us of the tears we cried when we were slaves.

Who am I? _____

3 I taste bitter. I am a reminder of our bitter lives as slaves.

Who am I? _____

4 I remind everyone of the bricks we had to make when we were slaves in Egypt.

Who am I? _____

5 I am a sweet liquid. I am poured into a glass four times during the seder. Each time reminds us of God's four promises to bring us from slavery to freedom.

Who am I? _____

שׁוֹפָר

Shofar

NEW LETTER
פ

LETTERS YOU KNOW. Say the name and sound of each letter.

ב כ ר ה ל מ שׁ ת ב

ם י ח נ ע צ ק ו א ד

ס פ ט

VOWELS YOU KNOW. Say the sound of each vowel.

וֹ י

FAY

פ

פֹ		פְ	פוֹ	פַ	פֶ	פִי 1
פֹ		פֹ	פַ	פַ	פְ	פֶ 2
צוֹפְ	תְּפָ	לְפָ	שָׁפַ	אֶפָ	נָפַ 3

SHAPE IT UP

What does **Fay** look like?
Close your eyes and picture the letter.
Draw it in the air or use your whole body to
make the shape of the letter **Fay**.

Make up a clue to remember **Fay**

_____ .

HEADS UP!

The letters פ and פ make different sounds.

What sound does פ make?
What sound does פ make?
How do they look different?

Make up a clue to help you remember the
difference between פ and פ.

_____

103

Read lines 1-4 in a soft voice. Read lines 5-8 in a regular voice.

1	יָפֶה	עָפָר	כַּפִּי	נֶפֶשׁ	חֹפֶשׁ	צוֹפֶה
2	אֹפִי	תָּפַס	נָפַל	אָפָה	יָפִים	נַפְשִׁי
3	אֹפֶן	אֶפֶס	צָפוֹן	שֶׁפַע	כֹּפֶר	יִפְתֶּה
4	אָסַפְתָּ	אֶפְשָׁר	תְּפִלָּה	מַפְטִיר	תִּפְתַּח	לִפְעָמִים
5	תְּפִלּוֹת	סְפָרִים	סוֹפְרִים	לְפָנִים	צוֹפִיָּה	אַפְקִיד
6	לִפְדוֹת	נוֹפְלִים	טוֹטָפֹת	נַפְשְׁכֶם	תִּפְאֶרֶת
7	אֲפִיקוֹמָן	הַפְטָרָה	שׁוֹפְטִים	כְּמִפְעָלוֹ	תְּפִילִין
8	שׁוֹפָר	תְּפִלָּה	תְּפִילִין	מַפְטִיר	הַפְטָרָה

I KNOW HEBREW!

Can you find these Hebrew words above?

prayer = תְּפִלָּה

Haftarah = הַפְטָרָה

shofar = שׁוֹפָר

soul = נֶפֶשׁ

afikoman = אֲפִיקוֹמָן

Read and circle or highlight them.

STRIKE A POSE

Show off your best שׁוֹפָר blowing stance!

Make the sound of a שׁוֹפָר too (if it's OK with everyone else in the room).

פ פּ

Write the Hebrew word for *shofar*.

שׁוֹפָר

Write the Hebrew word for *soul*.

נֶפֶשׁ

Write the Hebrew word for *prayer*.

תְּפִלָה

Write the Hebrew word for *afikoman*.

אֲפִיקוֹמָן

Write the Hebrew word for *Haftarah*.

הַפְטָרָה

PRAYER PRACTICE

Find the Hebrew letters on each line that sound the same as the English in the box.
Write the letters on the line or say them. Remember that some Hebrew letters sound alike.

ד	תָּמִיד מְסַפְּרִים כְּבוֹד אֱלֹהִים	D	1
	אֲשֶׁר אָנֹכִי מְצַוֶּה אֶתְכֶם הַיּוֹם	M	2
	עַל לְבַבְכֶם וְעַל נַפְשְׁכֶם	V	3
	נַפְשִׁי תִדּוֹם וְנַפְשִׁי כֶּעָפָר לַכֹּל תִּהְיֶה	F	4
	קְשַׁרְתֶּם אֹתָם לְאוֹת עַל יֶדְכֶם	T	5
	פּוֹתְחִים אֶת פִּיהֶם בְּשִׁירָה	P	6

105

OUR TRADITION — שׁוֹפָר

The שׁוֹפָר is made from a ram's horn. When it is blown, it makes a loud trumpeting sound.
In ancient times the שׁוֹפָר was blown to announce the beginning of Shabbat.
We blow the שׁוֹפָר on Rosh Hashanah and at the end of Yom Kippur.
On Rosh Hashanah the shofar is blown 100 times!

What do you think about or feel when you hear the sound of the שׁוֹפָר?

PICTURE PERFECT

Read each word aloud.
Match the correct word
with its picture.

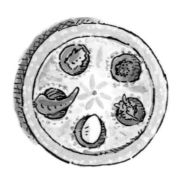

טַלִּית

תּוֹרָה

שׁוֹפָר

פֶּסַח

אֲרוֹן הַקֹּדֶשׁ

CHECKPOINT CHALLENGE

Show off your Hebrew reading skills!

Read aloud each word. Give yourself one point for every word read correctly.

4 דֶּלֶת	3 עֶבֶד	2 בֶּאֱמֶת	1 אֱלֹהִים
8 טֶרֶם	7 חֶסֶד	6 מִצְוָה	5 הֶבֶל
12 לֶחֶם	11 תֹּכֶן	10 כֶּתֶר	9 יִהְיֶה
16 עֶרֶב	15 סֶלַע	14 נֶאֱמָן	13 עֹמֶר
20 קֶרֶן	19 צֶדֶק	18 נֶפֶשׁ	17 פֶּסַח
24 תֶּבֶן	23 כֹּתֶל	22 אֲשֶׁר	21 פֶּרֶק

Earn another point for each word you can translate into English.

How did you do?

LESSON 19

עֵץ חַיִּים

Tree of Life

LETTERS YOU KNOW. Say the name and sound of each letter.

ב כ ר ה ה כּ ל מ שׁ ת תּ ב

ד א ו ק צ ע נ ן ח י ם

ט פ ס ף

VOWELS YOU KNOW. Say the sound of each vowel.

וֹ ‏ ִי

NEW LETTER

ץ

NEW VOWELS

ל

ל

---

1 נֵי דֵ לִי מֵי פֵּי שֵׁי

2 כֵ עֵי יֵי טֵי סֵ פֵּי

3 שְׂרֵי דְרֵי הֵיט אוֹמֵ כֹּה סֵף

Read the lines above. Which Hebrew sound reminds you of a horse?

Write it in Hebrew here:_____

SHAPE IT UP

What does ◻ sound like?
Make a hand motion to show the shape
of ◻ as you say its sound.

What does ◻ל sound like?
Make a hand motion to show the shape
of ◻ל as you say its sound.

108

Read aloud the lines below as if you were telling a story. Read lines 1-2 in a sad voice.
Read lines 3-4 in a happy voice. The scary part is on lines 5-6, and the exciting part is on line 7.
Line 8 is the last line of your "story." How will it end? You decide.

1	בֶּן	שֵׁם	יֵשׁ	אֵלִי	כֵּן	אִם
2	אֵין	בֵּית	נֵס	בֵּין	לֵב	נֵר
3	חֵטְא	אָמֵן	סֵדֶר	כָּשֵׁר	סֵפֶר	שְׁתֵּי
4	חָבֵר	אוֹמֵר	כֹּהֵן	הַלֵּל	דִּבֵּר	עֵדֶן
5	לִבְנֵי	תּוֹקֵעַ	הֵיטֵב	סוֹפֵר	רוֹפֵא	יוֹצֵר
6	אֱלֹהֵי	פִּרְקֵי	נִדְרֵי	אַחֲרֵי	חַסְדֵי	תִּשְׁרֵי
7	אָמֵן	לֵישֵׁב	בְּצֵאת	אוֹהֵב	מְקַדֵּשׁ	מַלְאֲכֵי
8	בְּרֵאשִׁית	סֵפֶר	תּוֹרָה	נֵר תָּמִיד	שָׁלוֹם עֲלֵיכֶם	

I KNOW HEBREW!

Can you find the Hebrew words above?

Torah scroll, Five Books of Moses = סֵפֶר תּוֹרָה

seder = סֵדֶר   **Eternal Light** = נֵר תָּמִיד

amen = אָמֵן   **heart** = לֵב

Read and circle or highlight them. Find the Hebrew word we say at the end of a prayer or blessing.

Which line is it on?_____

(Hint: It means "so be it." When you say this word, you are saying you agree with the prayer or blessing.)

RHYMETIME

Read aloud the words to the right. Circle or highlight the two on each line that rhyme. Sing the rhyming words aloud.

1	בֵּן	נֵר	תֵּל	כֵּן
2	אָמַר	אָמֵן	שָׁמֶן	עֹמֶר
3	קוֹרֵא	תּוֹקֵעַ	שׁוֹמֵר	שׁוֹמֵעַ
4	מִנְיָן	מִקְוֶה	בִּנְיָן	בָּנִים
5	טַהֵר	טוֹבָה	מַהֵר	מִצְוָה
6	תִּפְאֶרֶת	שַׁחֲרִית	אוֹמְרוֹת	סוֹפֶרֶת
7	צְדָקָה	רַחֲמִים	רַחֲמָן	צַדִּיקִים
8	מַלְאָכֵי	פְּעָמִים	פַּעֲמוֹן	פִּרְקֵי

FINAL TZADEE

ץ

1	עֵץ	קֵץ	חֵץ	רָץ	אָץ	נֵץ
2	עֵץ	עֵצִים	רָץ	רָצָה	לֵץ	לֵיצָן
3	צֵץ	צַע	רֵץ	פִּיץ	רֵן	צָה

SHAPE IT UP

What does **Final Tzadee** look like?
Close your eyes and picture the letter.
Draw it in the air or use your whole body to make the shape of the letter **Final Tzadee**.

Make up a clue to remember
Final Tzadee.

HEADS UP!

There are five letters in the Hebrew alphabet that have a different form when they come at the end of a word.

When a צ comes at the end of a word, it is a **Final** ץ.

Can you name two other letters that have a final form?

Read aloud the lines below. Then read again only the words that end with a **Final Tzadee**.

1	אֶרֶץ	חָמֵץ	מַצָּה	חָפֵץ	קַיִץ	אֹמֶץ
2	קוֹץ	קוֹצִים	בּוֹץ	פָּרַץ	קוֹפֵץ	קוֹפֶצֶת
3	נוֹצֵץ	לוֹחֵץ	צַנְחָן	עָצִיץ	מִיץ	נִמְצָץ
4	אֹמֶץ	אֶמְצַע	מֶרֶץ	אָמִיץ	הֵצִיץ	צִיֵן
5	לִקְפֹּץ	קְפִיצָה	קָמָץ	חוֹלֵץ	חוֹלֵם	הֵפִיץ
6	רוֹחֵץ	רָחֲצָה	יוֹעֵץ	צִפֹּרֶן	וֶאֱמַץ	פֶּרֶץ
7	לְשַׁבֵּץ	נִצְטַוָּה	צְבָעִים	מֵלִיץ	צָפוֹן	חָמִיץ
8	עֵץ חַיִּים	הַמּוֹצִיא לֶחֶם מִן הָאָרֶץ				

Great job!

I KNOW HEBREW!

Can you find these Hebrew words above?

Tree of Life = עֵץ חַיִּים

leavened food = חָמֵץ

Read and circle or highlight them.

Can you find the Hebrew word for the special food we eat during פֶּסַח?

Write it here. _____.

Does that word contain a **Tzadee** or a **Final Tzadee**?

ץ ^{¹ע ²} ץ

Write the Hebrew words for **Tree of Life**.

עֵץ חַיִּים עֵץ חַיִּים

Write the Hebrew word for **leavened food**.

חָמֵץ חָמֵץ

Write the Hebrew words for **Torah scroll**.

סֵפֶר תּוֹרָה סֵפֶר תּוֹרָה

Write the Hebrew words for **Eternal Light**.

נֵר תָּמִיד נֵר תָּמִיד

Write the Hebrew word for **seder**.

סֵדֶר סֵדֶר

Write the Hebrew word for **amen**.

אָמֵן אָמֵן

ADD A TZADEE

Complete each word below by adding the correct form of the letter **Tzadee**.
Then read all the words. When you read a word that contains a **Tzadee**, stand up. When you read a word that contains a **Final Tzadee**, sit down.

3 מִ‍ַ‍ָוָה	2 מַ‍ָ‍ה	1 עֵ‍ץ
6 דָקָה	5 חָמֵ‍	4 הָאָרֶ‍
9 קוֹפֵ‍	8 ‍ָוָה	7 בָּעִים
12 ‍ִדִיק	11 קָמַ‍	10 המוֹ‍ִיא

112

OUR TRADITION — עֵץ חַיִּים

A **Tree of Life**—עֵץ חַיִּים—is one of the symbols of the Torah.

In fact, the two wooden rollers around which the תּוֹרָה scroll is wrapped
are called עֲצֵי חַיִּים—trees of life. The תּוֹרָה is like a tree because just as a tree is strong
and offers food, so, too, the Torah gives the Jewish people strength and nourishes our souls.

How can the Torah give the Jewish people strength and nourishment?
Talk about it with a partner.

CONNECTIONS

Connect the beginning of a phrase with its ending. Say the phrase out loud.

עֲלֵיכֶם	יוֹם	6	נִשְׁתַּנָּה	הַמּוֹצִיא	1
טוֹבָה	אֲרוֹן	7	תּוֹרָה	מַה	2
הַקֹּדֶשׁ	נֵר	8	מִצְרַיִם	עֵץ	3
תָּמִיד	שָׁנָה	9	לֶחֶם	סֵפֶר	4
טוֹב	שָׁלוֹם	10	חַיִּים	יְצִיאַת	5

ALEF BET CHART

You have learned 5 new letters in Lessons 15-19:

צ   פ   ס   פּ   ט

Turn to the **Alef Bet** chart on page 160. Color in the new letters.

Can you say the name and sound of each letter you now know?

יִשְׂרָאֵל

Israel

NEW LETTER

שׂ

LETTERS YOU KNOW. Say the name and sound of each letter.

ב כ ר ה כ מ ל שׁ ת ת ב

ד א ו ק צ ע נ ן ח י ם

ט פ ס פ ץ

VOWELS YOU KNOW. Say the sound of each vowel.

וֹ י

SIN

שׂ

שָׂ	שֶׂ	שׂוֹ	שֵׂי	שִׂי	שָׂ	1
שׂוֹ	שׂוֹ	שׂי	שׂי	שֶׂ	שֵׂ	2
עֲשָׂ	יְשָׂ	שָׂפָ	שֵׁב שָׂשׂוֹ	מַשׂ		3

SHAPE IT UP

What does *Sin* look like?

Close your eyes and picture the letter.

Draw it in the air or use your whole body to make the shape of the letter *Sin*.

Make up a clue to remember *Sin*.

HEADS UP!

The letters שׂ and שׁ make different sounds.

What sound does שׁ make?

What sound does שׂ make?

How do they look different?

Make up a clue to help you remember the difference between שׂ and שׁ.

Read aloud all the words that start with **Sin**. Next, read all the words that have a **Sin** in the middle of the word. Then, read all the words that do not have a **Sin**.

1	שֶׂה	שִׂים	שַׂר	שָׂם	שַׂק	שִׂיא
2	שָׂרָה	שָׂנֵא	שָׂמַח	עֶשֶׂר	עָשָׂה	מַשָׂא
3	שָׂרָה	שָׂרָה	שָׂמָה	שָׂמָה	שַׂעַר	שָׂשׂוֹן
4	שֵׂעָר	שָׂכָר	שָׂפָה	יִשָׂא	בָּשָׂר	שֵׂכֶל
5	שָׂדֶה	פָּשַׁט	שֶׁבַע	עֶשֶׂר	עָשָׂה	תַּיִשׁ
6	שִׂמְחַת	תּוֹרָה	שְׁמוֹנֶה	עֲשָׂרָה	עֲשֶׂרֶת הַדִבְּרוֹת	
7	שְׁמַע	יִשְׂרָאֵל	שִׂים	שָׁלוֹם	עוֹשֶׂה	שָׁלוֹם
8	עַם	יִשְׂרָאֵל	בְּנֵי	יִשְׂרָאֵל	אֶרֶץ	יִשְׂרָאֵל

I KNOW HEBREW!

Can you find the Hebrew words above?

Ten Commandments = עֲשֶׂרֶת הַדִבְּרוֹת
Rejoicing of the Torah = שִׂמְחַת תּוֹרָה
Israel = יִשְׂרָאֵל

WORD RIDDLE

I am a holiday we celebrate each year when we finish reading the entire תּוֹרָה.

We then begin reading the תּוֹרָה from the very first word all over again.

My name begins with שׂ. What holiday am I?

115

PRAYER PRACTICE

The phrases below are all from prayers you may find in a siddur, a prayer book. Practice reading them. Write or say the number of words that have a *Sin* in each line.

שְׁמַע יִשְׂרָאֵל	1
שִׂים שָׁלוֹם טוֹבָה...בְּרָכָה	2
עוֹשֶׂה שָׁלוֹם...יַעֲשֶׂה שָׁלוֹם	3
בּוֹרֵא מִינֵי בְשָׂמִים	4
בְּלִי רֵאשִׁית בְּלִי תַכְלִית	5
וְאֵין שֵׁנִי לְהַמְשִׁיל לוֹ	6
לֹא תִשָּׂא אֶת שֵׁם (אֱלֹהִים)...לַשָּׁוְא	7
וַיִּשְׁבֹּת בַּיּוֹם הַשְּׁבִיעִי...מְלַאכְתּוֹ אֲשֶׁר עָשָׂה	8
לִשְׁמֹעַ לִלְמֹד...לְלַמֵּד לִשְׁמֹר וְלַעֲשׂוֹת	9
בַּיּוֹם הַשְּׁבִיעִי שָׁבַת וַיִּנָּפַשׁ	10

שׁ שׂ

Write the Hebrew word for **Israel**.

יִשְׂרָאֵל

Write the Hebrew words for **Rejoicing of the Torah**.

שִׂמְחַת תּוֹרָה

SOUNDS LIKE

Read aloud each line. Find the Hebrew sounds on each line that are the same.
Circle, say, or write them.

עַד אֵד	צֵד	(אֵד)	אֵם	(עַד)	1
	סַם	בֹּס	שָׁם	כֹּס	2
	צֵל	לוֹ	עוֹל	לֹא	3
	כְּכֹל	כֹּל	קוֹל	יָכוֹל	4
	תּוֹט	בֵּיתָה	טֶבֶת	תּוֹת	5
	אֲשֶׁר	אֹסֶה	עֹשֶׂר	עוֹשֶׂה	6
	בּוֹכֶה	בּוֹקֶר	קְפֵּר	כּוֹפֵר	7
	אָסִיתִי	עֲרָסוֹת	עֲרָסוֹת	עֲשִׂיתִי עֲשָׂרוֹת	8

HEADS UP!

The letters שׂ and ס make the same sound. What sound do they make?

117

OUR TRADITION – יִשְׂרָאֵל

Jewish people have lived in יִשְׂרָאֵל for more than 3,000 years.

It is the country where our ancestors Abraham and Sarah lived.
It is the country where King David ruled. יִשְׂרָאֵל is the country where the modern state of Israel, our homeland, was reborn. יִשְׂרָאֵל has a special place in the hearts of Jews around the world.

Have you or anyone you know visited יִשְׂרָאֵל?

TOURING יִשְׂרָאֵל

Below are the names of eight places in יִשְׂרָאֵל.

Read aloud the Hebrew name of each place.

Then look at the map of יִשְׂרָאֵל.

Write or say the matching number for each English name.

צְפַת	1
תֵּל-אָבִיב	2
אֵילַת	3
הֶרְצְלִיָּה	4
מְצָדָה	5
חֵיפָה	6
יְרוּשָׁלַיִם	7
בְּאֵר שֶׁבַע	8

Haifa · · Safed
Herzliya ·
Tel Aviv ·
· Jerusalem
Masada ·
Beersheba ·
Eilat ·

118

חַג שָׂמֵחַ

Happy Holiday

LETTERS YOU KNOW. Say the name and sound of each letter.

ב כ ר ה כ ל מ שׁ ת ת ב

ד א ו ק צ ע נ ן ח י ם

ט פ ס פ ץ שׂ

VOWELS YOU KNOW. Say the sound of each vowel.

וֹ ‏ ‏ ‏ ‏ ‏ ‏

‏ ‏ ‏ ‏ ‏

NEW LETTER

ג

גֵי	גַ	גֶ	גִי	גוֹ	גַ	1

GIMMEL

גִיר	גִיס	גַנִי	גַבֵּי	גַלוֹ	גַג	2

גוֹלָ	גְטִי	הָג	גָא	גְבוֹ	גֵּד	3

SHAPE IT UP

What does **Gimmel** look like?

Close your eyes and picture the letter.

Draw it in the air or use your whole body to make the shape of the letter **Gimmel**.

Make up a clue to remember **Gimmel**.

119

READY, SET, READ

Read aloud the lines below. Then give yourself a pat on the back.
Choose a line to read again to a partner. Ask your partner to decide how to let you know
if you did a good job. Then switch.

1	חַג	גַּן	גְּדִי	גֵּר	דָּג	גַּם
2	גֹּלֶם	גָּדֵל	מָגֵן	עֹנֶג	גֶּפֶן	גִּיל
3	גִּבּוֹר	גּוֹלֵל	גּוֹמֵל	גָּאַל	גֶּשֶׁם	דֶּגֶל
4	גּוֹלָה	מְגִלָּה	הִשִּׂיג	מִנְהָג	גָּדוֹל	גְּטִים
5	אַגָּדָה	אֶתְרֹג	רֶגֶל	הִגְדִּיל	חַגִּים	גְּדוֹלָה
6	גְּמָרָא	נָגִילָה	הִגִּיעַ	חֲגִיגָה	שִׁגָּעוֹן	פִּתְגָּם
7	מָגֵן	אַבְרָהָם	מְגִלָּה	עֹנֶג	שַׁבָּת	יִתְגַּדַל
8	הַגָּדָה	חַד גַּדְיָא	מָגֵן דָּוִד	מָגֵן אָבוֹת		

I KNOW HEBREW!

Can you find these Hebrew
words above?

scroll = מְגִלָּה

haggadah = הַגָּדָה

Shield of David,
Jewish Star = מָגֵן דָּוִד

Read and circle or highlight them.

EXTRA CREDIT

The Jewish star is known as the **Magen David**—the Shield of David.
David was an ancient king of Israel. We can see this symbol on the
flag of Israel. Can you find the Hebrew words for **Magen David** above?
Write the line number. _____

Do you know what the flag of Israel looks like?
Look for it on page 119, then draw it below.

120

I SPY

Read each line.

Find the Hebrew letter that sounds the same as the English in the box. Circle it.

						English	#
כ	פ	ב	כ	(ב)	ג	B	1
ל	ט	ח	מ	ס	צ	T	2
ם	ח	ס	ת	כ	ט	M	3
ו	כ	ד	ן	ע	ר	N	4
ת	מ	שׁ	ט	שׂ	ה	S	5
ז	י	ג	פ	נ	ו	V	6
ע	ו	י	צ	א	ז	Y	7
נ	ר	ל	ג	ו	ס	G	8
ז	ע	ק	א	שׁ	צ	TS	9
ב	פ	כ	ב	פ	ת	P	10

HEADS UP!

When ח comes at the end of a word, we read the vowel first and then the letter. שָׂמֵחַ sounds like שָׂמֵאַח.

						#
אֹחַ	שִׂיחַ	נֹחַ	רֵיחַ	מֹחַ	כֹּחַ	1
טִיחַ	כְּשִׂיחַ	לְנֹחַ	הַמֹּחַ	בַּכֹּחַ	יָרֵחַ	2
נֹוחַ	רֹחַ	גִּיחַ	שִׂיחַ	מִיחַ	רֵחַ	3

121

The first word on line 1, שָׂמֵחַ, means "happy." Read lines 1-4 in a happy voice. Read lines 5-8 in your regular voice, except when you come to the word שָׂמֵחַ. Read that word in a happy voice.

בַּכֹּחַ	מֵנִיחַ	נָשִׂיחַ	אוֹרֵחַ	יָרֵחַ	שָׂמֵחַ	1
לִפְתֹּחַ	פָּתַח	פּוֹתֵחַ	סוֹלֵחַ	פּוֹקֵחַ	מָשִׂיחַ	2
מַפְתֵּחַ	שָׁלִיחַ	מָנוֹחַ	שׁוֹלֵחַ	מְנַצֵּחַ	לְשַׁבֵּחַ	3
פּוֹרֵחַ	לִשְׂמֵחַ	לוֹקֵחַ	הִצְלִיחַ	מִשְׁלוֹחַ	מַצְמִיחַ	4
שָׂמֵחַ	מְשַׂמֵּחַ	שִׂיחָה	אָשִׂיחַ	הַשְׁגָּחָה	מַשְׁגִּיחַ	5
נִפְקַח	פְּקֵחַ	טָרַח	טוֹרֵחַ	בָּטַח	הִבְטִיחַ	6
סְלִיחָה	סָלַח	לִסְלֹחַ	בָּרַח	לִבְרֹחַ	בּוֹרֵחַ	7
מְגִלָּה	הַגָּדָה	פֶּסַח	שָׂמֵחַ	חַג	מָשִׂיחַ	8

I KNOW HEBREW!

Can you find the Hebrew words above?

happy holiday = חַג שָׂמֵחַ

moon = יָרֵחַ

Read and circle or highlight them.

PRAYER PRACTICE

The phrases below are all from prayers you may find in a siddur, a prayer book. Practice reading them aloud. Put a check next to the two lines you find most challenging.

1   לְשַׁבֵּחַ לַאֲדוֹן הַכֹּל

2   הָאֵל הַגָּדוֹל הַגִּבּוֹר וְהַנּוֹרָא

3   לְעֵת תָּכִין מַטְבֵּחַ

4   לְהוֹדוֹת לְהַלֵּל לְשַׁבֵּחַ

5   שְׂמֵחִים בְּצֵאתָם וְשָׂשִׂים בְּבֹאָם

6   מְשַׂמֵּחַ צִיּוֹן בְּבָנֶיהָ

SAY A BLESSING

Practice reading these endings to five different blessings, בְּרָכוֹת.

When do we recite each one? Write it on the blank lines.

1   בּוֹרֵא פְּרִי הַגָּפֶן

2   בּוֹרֵא פְּרִי הָעֵץ

3   בּוֹרֵא פְּרִי הָאֲדָמָה

4   בּוֹרֵא מְאוֹרֵי הָאֵשׁ

5   בּוֹרֵא מִינֵי בְשָׂמִים

THE ADDED DOT

Add a dot to one member of each set of family letters. Then say or write the sound of each letter.

ת ת   פ פ   כ כ   ב ב

_B_

___ ___   ___ ___   ___ ___

Which letter did not change its sound when you added a dot?

123

RHYMETIME

Read the Hebrew words below. Connect the rhyming words, then sing them out loud.

גּוֹמֵל	כֹּחַ	5	הַגָּדָה	רֶגֶל	1
טָהֹר	יָרֵחַ	6	סוֹלֵחַ	מָשִׁיחַ	2
שָׂמֵחַ	גּוֹלֵל	7	דֶּגֶל	אַגָּדָה	3
מֹחַ	גִּבּוֹר	8	שָׁלִיחַ	פּוֹקֵחַ	4

WRITING PRACTICE

גּ גּ גּ

Write the Hebrew words for **happy holiday**.

חַג שָׂמֵחַ

Write the Hebrew word for **haggadah**.

הַגָּדָה

Write the Hebrew word for **scroll**.

מְגִלָּה

Write the Hebrew words for **Shield of David**.

מָגֵן דָּוִד

124

OURTRADITION — חַג שָׂמֵחַ

The word חַג means "holiday" or "festival." The word שָׂמֵחַ means "happy" or "joyous."

When we say חַג שָׂמֵחַ, we wish someone a happy holiday.

Name a holiday when you might say חַג שָׂמֵחַ.

WORD WIZARD

Follow the directions to discover a hidden phrase.

Cross out the Hebrew letters and their vowels that match the English sounds.

Write the remaining Hebrew letters and their vowels.

1

1 SAY	4 M	7 SHOH
2 TEH	5 PEH	8 GEH
3 NEE	6 VEE	9 HAH

סִיחַטְנִיגם   פְּשָׁוְימֶשׁוֹגֵחַה

_____ _____

_____ _____

What does it mean? _____

When do we use it? _____

2

1 YAH	4 SAH	7 KAH
2 FOH	5 N	8 EH
3 CHAH	6 GEE	9 DAY

יַפוֹשַׁחַבַּשָׁתן   גִיקָשָׁעֲלוֹדִים

_____ _____

_____ _____

What does it mean? _____

When do we use it? _____

CHECKPOINT CHALLENGE

Play Tic-Tac-Toe with a partner. If you read the word correctly, mark the square with an X or an O.

אֵין	בֵּית-כְּנֶסֶת	חָבֵר
מָגֵן	קַדֵּשׁ	כֹּהֵן
וֵאלֹהֵי	חֵטְא	טֵבֵת
יֵצֶר	כֵּן	מַלְאֲכֵי
הַלֵּל	מֵבִין	נֵרוֹת
סֵפֶר	עֵדֶן	פֵּרוֹת
סוֹפֵר	יוֹצֵר	פִּרְקֵי
בּוֹרֵא	שֵׁם	שֵׂכֶל
תֵּשַׁע	מֹשֶׁה	שָׂמֵחַ

קָדוּשׁ

Kiddush

LETTERS YOU KNOW. Say the name and sound of each letter.

ב כ ר ה כ ל מ שׁ ת ת ב

ם י ח ן ע צ ק ו א ד

ג שׂ ץ פ ס פּ ט

VOWELS YOU KNOW. Say the sound of each vowel.

וֹ יִ

יֵ

NEW VOWEL

וּ

וּ

צוּ	מוּ	נוּ	טוּ	שׁוּ	סוּ		1
תֻ	קֻ	רֻ	שֻׁ	גֻ	בֻּ		2
כֻּלוֹ	צוּד	בָּנוּ	אָנוּ	לָנוּ	הוּא		3

SHAPE IT UP

What does וּ sound like?
Make a hand motion to show the shape of וּ as you say its sound.

What does ֻ sound like?
Make a hand motion to show the shape of ֻ as you say its sound.

What is the sound a cow makes? Write it in Hebrew here:_____

What sound is the opposite of "old"? Write it in Hebrew here:_____

127

Read aloud the lines below. Point to your belly when you read an "oo" vowel sound.

1 חָמֵשׁ לוּחַ כֻּלָּם וְהָיוּ סֻכָּה טֵבוּ

2 עָלֵינוּ לִבֵּנוּ סֻכּוֹת שָׁבוּעַ חֲנֻכָּה קִבּוּץ

3 קָדוֹשׁ שֻׁלְחָן מְשֻׁבָּח סִדּוּר מְצֻיָּן כֻּלָּנוּ

4 הַלְלוּיָהּ גְּדֻלָּה פָּסוּק יְשׁוּעָה נְטוּיָה אֲנַחְנוּ

5 וּבְנֵחָה לוּלָב וְיָפֻצוּ וַיְכֻלּוּ וַיְנַסּוּ דַּיֵּנוּ

6 תְּמוּנָה וְצִוָּנוּ אֵלִיָּהוּ הַנָּבִיא בָּרְכוּ קָשִׁיּוֹת

7 קְדֻשָּׁה יְהוּדִים פּוּרִים יוֹם כִּפּוּר שָׁבוּעוֹת

8 יְרוּשָׁלַיִם אֱלֹהֵינוּ שֶׁהֶחֱיָנוּ אָבִינוּ מַלְכֵּנוּ

I KNOW HEBREW!

Can you find these Hebrew words above?

The Five Books of Moses = חָמֵשׁ
Jerusalem = יְרוּשָׁלַיִם
Elijah the Prophet = אֵלִיָּהוּ הַנָּבִיא
Kiddush = קָדוֹשׁ
prayer book = סִדּוּר
Jews = יְהוּדִים

Read and circle or highlight them.

EXTRA CREDIT

Can you find the Hebrew word for *prayer book* in the lines above?

Write it here:

_____

I SPY

Read aloud each line.

Find the Hebrew that sounds the same as the English in the box. Circle it or highlight it.

1	SHOO	שָׁ	(שׁוּ)	שׁוּ	שִׁי	שָׁ	שָׁי
2	FOH	פוּ	פָ	פִ	פּוֹ	פְ	פֵי
3	AH	עִ	עֲ	עִ	עַ	עֲ	עוּ
4	SEE	שָׁ	שְׁ	שׁוֹ	שֶׁ	שַׁ	שִׁי
5	YOH	יֹן	יְ	יׄ	יִי	יִי	יְ
6	PEH	פְ	פַ	פֶ	פּוֹ	פֵי	פִי
7	TSOO	צֵי	צָ	צוּ	צֶ	צִ	צֹ
8	SOO	סַ	סוֹ	סֶ	סִי	סֹ	סֵ
9	EH	אִי	אוּ	אָ	אֶ	אֱ	אֹ
10	TAY	טוֹ	טַ	טְ	טֵי	טִ	טֹ

POWER READING

Practice reading these prayer phrases from the קִדּוּשׁ, which we recite over wine.

Write the number of words with the vowel וּ you find on each line.

1	אֲשֶׁר קִדְּשָׁנוּ בְּמִצְוֹתָיו וְרָצָה בָנוּ
2	וְשַׁבָּת...בְּאַהֲבָה וּבְרָצוֹן הִנְחִילָנוּ
3	כִּי הוּא יוֹם תְּחִלָּה לְמִקְרָאֵי קֹדֶשׁ
4	כִּי בָנוּ בָחַרְתָּ וְאוֹתָנוּ קִדַּשְׁתָּ
5	בְּאַהֲבָה וּבְרָצוֹן הִנְחַלְתָּנוּ
6	מְקַדֵּשׁ הַשַּׁבָּת

Write the Hebrew words for **the Five Books of Moses**.

חֻמָשׁ

Write the Hebrew word for **Jews**.

יְהוּדִים

Write the Hebrew word for **Jerusalem**.

יְרוּשָׁלַיִם

Write the Hebrew word for **prayer book**.

סִדּוּר

Write the Hebrew word for **Kiddush**.

קִדּוּשׁ

Write the Hebrew words for **Elijah the Prophet**.

אֵלִיָּהוּ הַנָּבִיא

PRAYER PRACTICE

Practice reading these siddur words with a partner. Take turns choosing a word for each of you to read.

וְשַׂמְּחֵנוּ	שָׂבְּעֵנוּ	קִדְּשָׁנוּ	וְצִוָּנוּ
וְהַגִּיעָנוּ	וְקִיְּמָנוּ	שֶׁהֶחֱיָינוּ	עָלֵינוּ
מַלְכֵּנוּ	אָבִינוּ	אֲבוֹתֵינוּ	אֱלֹהֵינוּ
עֵינֵינוּ	יִשְׁעֵנוּ	הָיִינוּ	גּוֹאֲלֵנוּ

HEADS UP!

All the words above end in נוּ. נוּ is a suffix that means "us" or "our."

The word אֲנַחְנוּ means "we."

Why do you think so many words in our prayers end with the suffix נוּ?

OUR TRADITION — קָדוֹשׁ

On Friday evening, after we light שַׁבָּת candles, we sing the קָדוֹשׁ over wine.
The word קָדוֹשׁ means "making holy." When we sing the קָדוֹשׁ prayer
we thank God for making שַׁבָּת a holy day.

The ark where we place the Torah is called the Holy Ark. We call Jerusalem the Holy City,
and Israel the Holy Land. Why do you think they are all holy?
What or who else do you think is holy?

HOLIDAY QUIZ

Read the name of each holiday. Use the word bank to answer the questions below.

יוֹם כִּפּוּר	פּוּרִים	סֻכּוֹת
שָׁבוּעוֹת		חֲנֻכָּה

1 We read the מְגִלָה. What holiday am I? _____

2 We shake the *lulav* and eat in a small booth. What holiday am I? _____

3 We celebrate the giving of the Torah. What holiday am I? _____

4 We light the *hanukkiyah*. What holiday am I? _____

5 We do not eat all day. What holiday am I? _____

מְזוּזָה

Mezuzah

NEW LETTER

ז

LETTERS YOU KNOW. Say the name and sound of each letter.

ב כ ר ה כ ל מ שׁ ת תּ בּ

ד א ו ק צ ע נ ן ח י ם

ט פּ ס פ ץ שׂ ג

VOWELS YOU KNOW. Say the sound of each vowel.

וֹ ִי ֵ ֶ ֲ ָ ַ

ֻ וּ ִי ֵ ְ ֳ

ZAYIN

זֵי	זִ	זְ	זִ	זוֹ	זוּ	זַ	1
צְ	זִ	סַ	זַ	שֵׁ	זֵ	2
זוֹר	זֶן	זֶ	יִז	זַר	זָוִי	חַז	3

Which Hebrew sound reminds you of a place to see lots of animals?

SHAPE IT UP

What does *Zayin* look like?
Close your eyes and picture the letter.
Draw it in the air or use your whole body to
make the shape of the letter *Zayin*.

HEADS UP!

The Hebrew letters ז, ס, צ, and שׂ make similar sounds.

What sound does each letter make?
Read each word carefully.

זְמַן חֶסֶד מִצְוָה שִׂמְחָה

132

Read aloud all the words that start with a **Zayin**. Then read all the words that end with a **Zayin**.
Are there words left? Read those too.

זָר	בּוּז	פָּז	עֹז	אָז	זֶה	1
אָחַז	חַזָן	חָזָק	אֹזֶן	זְמַן	זָכֹר	2
זָהָב	זָקֵן	מַזָל	זֹאת	זֶבַח	הַזָן	3
וְזַרְעוֹ	עֲזָנוּ	אֵיזֶה	זֵכֶר	מָעוֹז	יִזְכֹּר	4
זָוִית	נֶעֱזָב	מִזְמוֹר	מַחֲזוֹר	מִזְבֵּחַ	זִכָּרוֹן	5
עִזִים	זַרְעָם	מָזוֹן	זְרוֹעַ	מִזְרָח	זְכוּת	6
וֶאֱמַץ	חֲזַק	הִזְנִיחַ	זָקוּק	הֶחֱזִיר	זַיִת	7
טוֹב	מַזָל	מַחֲזוֹר	הַזִכָּרוֹן	יוֹם	מְזוּזָה	8

Say מַזָל טוֹב! **That means "congratulations"!**

I KNOW HEBREW!

Can you find these Hebrew
words above?

mezuzah = מְזוּזָה
mahzor = מַחֲזוֹר

Read and circle or highlight them.

PRAYER PRACTICE

Practice reading these siddur phrases. Look for *Zayin*s as you read. Write the number of words that have a *Zayin* on each line.

הַזָּן אֶת הַכֹּל	_____	1
זִכָּרוֹן לְמַעֲשֵׂה בְרֵאשִׁית	_____	2
זֵכֶר לִיצִיאַת מִצְרַיִם	_____	3
עֵץ חַיִּים הִיא לַמַּחֲזִיקִים בָּהּ	_____	4
וְלוֹ הָעֹז וְהַמִּשְׂרָה	_____	5
אָז אֶגְמֹר בְּשִׁיר מִזְמוֹר	_____	6
וּכְתַבְתָּם עַל מְזוּזוֹת	_____	7
עוֹזֵר וּמוֹשִׁיעַ וּמָגֵן	_____	8
בַּיָּמִים הָהֵם בַּזְּמַן הַזֶּה	_____	9
שֶׁהֶחֱיָנוּ וְקִיְּמָנוּ וְהִגִּיעָנוּ לַזְּמַן הַזֶּה	_____	10

I SPY

Read aloud the Hebrew words on each line. Circle or highlight the letter in each word that sounds like the English in the box.

שִׂמְחָה	שֵׂכֶל	יִשְׂרָאֵל	פּוֹרֵשׂ	S	1
גְּזֵרָה	זוֹרֵחַ	מַזָּל	יִזְכֹּר	Z	2
מִזְבֵּחַ	לַמְנַצֵּחַ	הִצְלִיחַ	מָשִׁיחַ	ACH	3
גֶּשֶׁם	מְגִלָּה	הַגָּדָה	גְּמָרָא	G	4
קִבּוּץ	וְאֶמַּץ	חָמֵץ	אֶרֶץ	TS	5
וְזַרְעוֹ	וְזֹאת	זוּג	זִיו	V	6

זֶ זֶ ז

Write the Hebrew word for **mezuzah**.

מְזוּזָה מְזוּזָה

Write the Hebrew words for **congratulations**.

מַזָּל טוֹב מַזָּל טוֹב

Write the Hebrew word for **machzor**.

מַחֲזוֹר מַחֲזוֹר

NAME TAG

Read the name of each letter in the box. Find its matching Hebrew letter and write it on the line. What sound does the letter make?

פ		ב	ס	פ	ת	כ	PAY	1
		ע	שׁ	צ	שׁ	ל	SIN	2
		ן	ד	נ	ו	ג	GIMMEL	3
		פ	ב	ת	כ	פ	FAY	4
		ק	שׁ	ס	צ	ם	SAMECH	5
		ט	ע	ת	ד	מ	TET	6
		נ	ו	ח	י	ר	YUD	7
		כ	ח	ג	ת	ה	HET	8
		נ	ו	ד	י	ג	NUN	9
		ס	שׁ	ג	ז	צ	ZAYIN	10

OUR TRADITION – מְזוּזָה

The Hebrew word for "doorpost" is מְזוּזָה. The תּוֹרָה teaches that the שְׁמַע and the וְאָהַבְתָּ prayers should be placed "on the doorposts of your house and on your gates."

That is why we write the words of these prayers on a piece of parchment and place them inside the מְזוּזָה, which is attached to the doorposts of our homes. מְזוּזָה is the Hebrew word for doorpost

Why do you think the תּוֹרָה teaches us to place the words of the שְׁמַע on the doorposts of our homes?

BE AN ARTIST

Draw a picture to illustrate each Hebrew word or phrase below.
If you want to check what the words mean, look at the מִילוֹן, the dictionary, on page 159.

טַלִית

סִדוּר

עֲשֶׂרֶת הַדִבְּרוֹת

נֵר תָּמִיד

CHECKPOINT CHALLENGE

Play Tic-Tac-Toe with a partner. Take turns reading a word.
If you read a word correctly, mark the square with an X or an O.

שָׁבוּעַ	יִרְבּוּ	גְּאוּלָה
אֵלִיָּהוּ	קְדוֹשׁ	סְגֻלָּה
חֻמָּשׁ	מְזוּזָה	צַו
כֻּלָּם	סִיּוּם	טוּבוֹ
תַּלְמוּד	הַלְלוּיָהּ	בָּרְכוּ
עֲצוּ	סֻכּוֹת	חֲנֻכָּה
צוּר	רְפוּאָה	פּוּרִים
שׁוּבָה	יְרוּשָׁלַיִם	קוּמוּ
זַיִת	מְתֻקָּן	שִׂישׂוּ

בָּרוּךְ

Praised, Blessed

LETTERS YOU KNOW. Say the name and sound of each letter.

ב כ ר ה כ ל מ שׁ תּ ת בּ

ם י ח ן ע צ ק א ו ד

ז שׁ ג צ פּ ס פ ט

VOWELS YOU KNOW. Say the sound of each vowel.

וֹ י ☐ ☐ ☐ ☐ ☐ ☐
                 ·   ·   ֱ   ְ   ָ   ַ

וּ י ☐ ☐ ☐ ☐ ☐
ֳ   ֻ   ֵ   ֶ   ·

NEW LETTER
ךְ

FINAL CHAF

1 רַךְ כַּךְ בָּךְ לֶךְ לְךָ וֵלֶךְ

2 אַךְ בְּךָ בְּךָ שֶׁלְךָ בְּכָךְ שִׁמְךָ תֶּיךָ

SHAPE IT UP

What does *Final Chaf* look like?
Close your eyes and picture the letter.

Draw it in the air or use your whole body to
make the shape of the letter *Final Chaf*.

Make up a clue to remember *Final Chaf*."

HEADS UP!

Final ךְ is the only final letter that
always has a vowel. Read these words.

הַמְבֹרָךְ   בֵּיתֶךָ

READING RULE When יךְ comes at the end of a word, the י is silent.

Read aloud each word that ends with a vowel sound ךָ.
Then read aloud each word that ends with ךְ.

עָלֶיךָ	דֶּרֶךְ	עַמְּךָ	שְׁמֶךָ	אִמְּךָ	בָּרוּךְ	1
לִבֵּךְ	אֶרֶךְ	פֶּרֶךְ	רֵעֲךָ	לִבְּךָ	מֶלֶךְ	2
עֻזֶּךָ	אָבִיךָ	אֵלֶיךָ	הוֹלֵךְ	צָרִיךְ	כָּמוֹךְ	3
כֻּלְּךָ	אוֹתְךָ	בֵּיתֶךָ	עִמְּךָ	בָּנֶיךָ	בָּרוּךְ	4
חֻקֶּיךָ	מְאֹדֶךָ	יָדֶיךָ	לְבָבְךָ	יִמְלֹךְ	מְבֹרָךְ	5
מַלְאָךְ	סוֹמֵךְ	מִצַוְּךָ	נַפְשְׁךָ	עֵינֶיךָ	לְפָנֶיךָ	6
וַיְבָרֶךְ	אֱלֹהַיִךְ	בִּשְׁלוֹמֶךָ	קָדְשָׁתֶךָ	בָּרוּךְ		7
וּבִשְׁעָרֶיךָ	וּבְקוּמֶךָ	וּבְלֶכְתְּךָ	מִצְוֹתֶיךָ	תַּנָךְ		8

I KNOW HEBREW!

Can you find these
Hebrew words above?

praised, blessed = בָּרוּךְ

king, ruler = מֶלֶךְ

Read and circle or highlight them.

EXTRA CREDIT

Perhaps you've heard a song
about a מֶלֶךְ named דָּוִד.
Can you sing the song and/or do the
hand motions that go along with it?

Ask a partner to do it with you!

CLIMB THE LADDERS

Climb up **Ladder Alef** by reading words 1-7.
Have your partner climb down **Ladder Bet** by reading words 8-14.
Climb up **Ladder Gimmel** by reading words 15-21. Have your partner climb down **Ladder Dalet** by reading words 22-28. Climbing can be tiring, so make sure to rest in between!

LADDER ד	LADDER ג	LADDER ב	LADDER א
22 אֱלֹהֶיךָ	21 מֶלֶךְ	8 כֶּתֶר	7 כֹּהֵן
23 בָּרוּךְ	20 שֵׂכֶל	9 כֻּלָּם	6 כְּפוֹר
24 לְךָ	19 חֲנֻכָּה	10 כַּוָּנָה	5 כָּבוֹד
25 עַמְּךָ	18 יָכְלוּ	11 עַכְשָׁו	4 כָּשֵׁר
26 דֶּרֶךְ	17 לִכְבוֹד	12 סֻכּוֹת	3 כֹּל
27 לְבָבְךָ	16 בֵּית-כְּנֶסֶת	13 בְּרָכוֹת	2 כּוֹס
28 נַפְשְׁךָ	15 יָכוֹל	14 יִזְכֹּר	1 כַּלָּה

HEADS UP!

There are five letters in the Hebrew alphabet that have a different form when they come at the end of a word.

When a כ comes at the end of a word, it is a final ךְ.

Can you name three other letters that have a final form?

ר דּ

Write the Hebrew word for **praised, blessed**.

בָּרוּךְ בָּרוּךְ

Write the Hebrew word for **king, ruler**.

מֶלֶךְ מֶלֶךְ

RHYME TIME

Read aloud each line. Three words on each line rhyme. Find the word that does not rhyme and write it on the line. Then snap or clap as you read aloud only the rhyming words.

שֶׁלְּךָ	אֶרֶךְ	(שֶׁלְּךָ)	מֶלֶךְ	דֶּרֶךְ	1
	יָדֶךָ	בֵּיתֶךָ	בָּרוּךְ	קוּמֶךָ	2
	אָרוֹךְ	מִצַּוְּךָ	לְבָבְךָ	נַפְשְׁךָ	3
	לְבָבֶךָ	מְבֹרָךְ	בְּבֵיתֶךָ	מְאֹדֶךָ	4
	לְכְתְּךָ	דַרְכְּךָ	עָלֶיךָ	שִׁבְתְּךָ	5
	עֵינֶיךָ	שְׁעָרֶיךָ	מַעֲשֶׂיךָ	שְׁלוֹמֶךָ	6

OUR TRADITION — בָּרוּךְ

We have a special way of saying "thank you" to God for God's gifts to us, by saying a בְּרָכָה.
The word בָּרוּךְ, which means "blessed" or "praised," is the first word of many blessings.

Below are the six words that begin many of the blessings we recite.
Read aloud these words, and then read the concluding phrases that follow.

בָּרוּךְ אַתָּה, יְיָ אֱלֹהֵינוּ, מֶלֶךְ הָעוֹלָם...

Praised are you, Adonai our God, Ruler of the world....

who brings forth bread from the earth.	הַמּוֹצִיא לֶחֶם מִן הָאָרֶץ.	1
who creates the fruit of the vine.	בּוֹרֵא פְּרִי הַגָּפֶן.	2
who creates the fruit of the earth.	בּוֹרֵא פְּרִי הָאֲדָמָה.	3
who creates the fruit of the tree.	בּוֹרֵא פְּרִי הָעֵץ.	4
who creates many kinds of food.	בּוֹרֵא מִינֵי מְזוֹנוֹת.	5
by whose word all things come into being.	שֶׁהַכֹּל נִהְיֶה בִּדְבָרוֹ.	6
for keeping us in life, for sustaining us, and for helping us to reach this day.	שֶׁהֶחֱיָנוּ וְקִיְּמָנוּ וְהִגִּיעָנוּ לַזְּמַן הַזֶּה.	7

SHOW WHAT YOU KNOW

Put a ⭐ next to the blessing you would say over חַלָה.

Put a ✔ next to the blessing you would say over wine or grape juice.

List three foods for which would you use the blessing that ends "who creates the fruit of the earth." Draw them here:

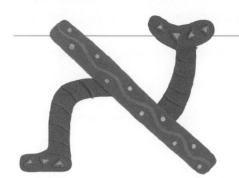

אָלֶף

Alef

LETTERS YOU KNOW. Say the name and sound of each letter.

ב כ ר ה ה ש ת מ ל כ ש ת ב

ם י ח ן ע נ צ ק ו א ד

ך ז ג שׂ ץ פ ס פּ ט

VOWELS YOU KNOW. Say the sound of each vowel.

וֹ ִי

ֱ ְ ֶ ֵ ָ ַ

וּ ֵי

ֲ ֳ ֹ ֺ

NEW LETTER

ף

סוֹף	גוּף	קוֹף	עוֹף	דַף	אַף	1
כֶּף	תַּף	סוֹף	עָף	תוֹף	כַּף	2
צוּף	רַף	סָף	טֶף	נָף	יֶף	3

FINAL FAY

ף

SHAPE IT UP

What does **Final Fay** look like?

Close your eyes and picture the letter.

Draw it in the air or use your whole body to make the shape of the letter **Final Fay**.

Make up a clue to remember **Final Fay**.

HEADS UP!

When a פ comes at the end of a word, it is a **Final** ף.

There are five letters in the Hebrew alphabet that have a different form when they come at the end of a word.

Name the other four letters that have a final form.

143

The letter **Final Fay** makes the sound of the English letter **F**. Read lines 1-3 to a **f**riend in a **f**unny voice. Read lines 4-6 in a **f**rightened voice. Read lines 7-8 in a **f**ancy voice.

חוֹף	סַף	עָיֵף	חַף	הַדַף	נוֹף	1
שָׂרַף	כֶּסֶף	עָנָף	עֶרֶף	תֵּיכֶף	חֹרֶף	2
כָּפַף	כָּתֵף	חָלַף	אֶלֶף	יוֹסֵף	שֶׁטֶף	3
לָעוּף	קוֹטֵף	זוֹקֵף	קָלַף	צָפוּף	מוּסַף	4
יָחֵף	כָּנָף	רָצוּף	שָׁטוּף	נִשְׂרַף	אָסַף	5
כְּפוּפִים	זוֹקֵף	שָׁלוֹם	רוֹדֵף	מְרַחֵף	עַפְעַף	6
לְשַׁפְשֵׁף	הֶחֱלִיף	לֶאֱסֹף	לְהִתְאַסֵף	מְצַפְצֵף		7
בַּצִיצִית	לְהִתְעַטֵף	וְצִוָּנוּ	בֵּית	אָלֶף		8

I KNOW HEBREW!

Can you find these Hebrew words above?

alef = אָלֶף

alef bet = אָלֶף בֵּית

Read and circle or highlight them.

EXTRA CREDIT

Can you find the Hebrew name for Joseph in the lines above? (Hint: The Hebrew name for Joseph begins with the letter **Yud**.)

Tell a partner what you know about the story of Joseph, the son of רָחֵל and יַעֲקֹב.

Can you find the Hebrew word for peace in the lines above?

Write it in Hebrew here:

_____

READING RELAY

In column א, Player 1 reads word 1. Player 2 reads words 1 and 2. Player 3 reads words 1, 2, and 3.
Continue the relay until all ten words in the column have been read.
Then repeat the Reading Relay with the words in columns ב and ג.

ג		ב		א	
ף		**פ פ**		**פ**	
כָּנָף	21	אֲפִיקוֹמָן	11	פָּסוּק	1
אָלֶף	22	שׁוֹפָר	12	פּוֹקֵחַ	2
קְלַף	23	גֶּפֶן	13	פִּרְקָן	3
יוֹסֵף	24	סֵפֶר	14	פְּעָמִים	4
רוֹדֵף	25	תְּפִלָה	15	פָּרָשָׁה	5
מְרַחֵף	26	מַפְטִיר	16	פּוּרִים	6
מוּסָף	27	תְּפִילִין	17	פֶּסַח	7
זוֹקֵף	28	לְפָנֵי	18	פְּרִי	8
תֵּיכֶף	29	מִשְׁפָּחָה	19	פֶּרֶךְ	9
אָסָף	30	תַּפּוּחַ	20	פָּנִים	10

EXTRA CREDIT

Can you find the Hebrew word for **afikoman**? Write it in Hebrew here:_____

Can you find the Hebrew word for **Passover**? Write it in Hebrew here:_____

פּ ףּ ף
₂⌐ →¹

Write the Hebrew word for **alef**.

אָלֶף   אָלֶף

Write the Hebrew words for **alef bet**.

אָלֶף בֵּית   אָלֶף בֵּית

I SPY

Read each line. Circle or highlight the Hebrew letters that sound the same as the English in the box.
Write the Hebrew letters on the line.

ךּ	מַלְכוּתְךָ	תְּפִילִין	לְפָנֶיךָ	סוֹמֵךְ	CH	1
	זוֹכֵר	כָּמֹכָה	בְּתוֹכֵנוּ	כָּבוֹד	CH	2
	אֲפִיקוֹמָן	פָּנִים	תְּפִלָּה	מַפְטִיר	F	3
	זוֹקֵף	מוּסָף	בָּרוּךְ	רוֹדֵף	F	4
	הִתְפַּלֵּל	מְפַרְנֵס	כְּפוּפִים	נוֹפְלִים	M	5
	טוּבוֹ	שְׁמוֹ	מִשְׁפָּטִים	מַצוֹת	M	6
	מָזוֹן	הַזָּן	אֶרֶץ	רָצוֹן	N	7
	אָבִי	מִנְיָן	נַפְשְׁךָ	נֶאֱמָן	N	8
	עָצִיץ	יַחַץ	אָמֵן	חָמֵץ	TS	9
	צְבָאָם	עֶלְיוֹן	צִיּוֹן	יִצְחָק	TS	10

HEADS UP!

Five Hebrew letters have final forms. Write the final form of each letter.

פ   כ   צ   מ   נ

OUR TRADITION — אָלֶף

אָלֶף is the name of the first letter in the Hebrew alphabet. The second letter in the Hebrew alphabet is בֵּית. That is why the name of the Hebrew alphabet is אָלֶף בֵּית.

When we know the letters of the אָלֶף בֵּית, we can read Hebrew words,
we can study the Torah, and we can pray from a סִדוּר.

How does it feel to know that you can read and write all the Hebrew letters and vowels?
Write a few of them here.

LETTER NAMES The names of the first ten letters of the אָלֶף בֵּית are in the correct order. The letters at the top are all mixed up. Write the correct letter above its name.

ז	ב	ט	ד	ו	י	ה	א	ח	ג
							א		
הֵא		דָלֶת		גִימֶל		בֵּית		אָלֶף	
יוּד		טֵית		חֵית		זַיִן		וָו	

ALEF BET CHART

You have learned five new letters in Lessons 20-25.

ק   ך   ז   ג   שׁ

Turn to the אָלֶף בֵּית chart on page 160. Color in the new letters.

You have learned every letter in the אָלֶף בֵּית. Recite the complete אָלֶף בֵּית. וּמַזָל טוֹב!

Give yourself a pat on the back. . . you deserve it!!

RULE #1

אִ ָ לִ ֶ לִ ָ אִ

When ֶ , ָ , or אֶ are followed by the letter י at the end of a word, say "EYE" as in "shy" (שַׁי).

אוּלַי	סִינַי	דַי	שַׁי	אֲזַי	חַי	1
בְּוַדַאי	הַלְוַאי	שַׁדַי	שְׂפָתַי	מָתַי	אֵלַי	2
רַבּוֹתַי	חֻקוֹתַי	מִצְוֹתַי	בְּחַיַי	אֱלֹהַי	אֲדֹנָי	3

I KNOW HEBREW!

Find this Hebrew word above.

Live = חַי

Read and circle or highlight it.

HEADS UP!

When וֹ comes after a letter that already has a vowel, it appears like וֹ and is pronounced "VOH."

מִצְוֹת = מִצְוֹת

מִצְוֹתַי = מִצְוֹתַי

RULE #2

ךְ

The dot in ךְ tells us it is a **Final kaf**. There are a few words in the siddur that end with ךְ, pronounced "KAH." Reading the following siddur words.

יִסְעָדֶךָ	וִיחֻנֶּךָ	אֲבָרֶכְךָ	וָאֲחַלְּצֶךָ	אוֹדֶךָ

RULE #3

יָיךְ יִךָ

When יִךָ, יָיךְ or יִךָ come at the end of a word, the letter י is silent.

1	חֲסָדֶיךָ	עֵינֶיךָ	נְסֶיךָ	לְפָנָיו	אֵלָיו	דְּבָרָיו
2	וּבִשְׁעָרֶיךָ	לְבָנֶיךָ	אֱלֹהֶיךָ	מַעֲשֶׂיךָ	עֲבָדֶיךָ	
3	בְּמִצְוֹתָיו	בִּמְרוֹמָיו	אֱלֹהָיו	רַחֲמָיו	מִצְוֹתָיו	

Can you find these Hebrew words above? Read and circle or highlight them.

With God's commandments = בְּמִצְוֹתָיו

Your kindnesses = חֲסָדֶיךָ

RULE #4

וֹי וּי

When the vowel וֹ is followed by the letter י at the end of a word, say "OY" as in "boy."

When the vowel וּ is followed by the letter י at the end of a word, say "OOEY" as in "gooey."

1	אוֹי	גוֹי	נוֹי	הוֹי	אֲבוֹי	כּוֹי
2	צִווּי	קָנוּי	עָשׂוּי	רָצוּי	גָּלוּי	וִדּוּי
3	פָּנוּי	עִלּוּי	בָּנוּי	רָאוּי	שָׁבוּי	

149

RULE #5	In the prayer book and in the Torah, God's name is written
יְיָ יְהֹוָה	יְהֹוָה, יְיָ, or אֲדֹנָי.
	We pronounce God's name "Adonai" (אֲדֹנָי).

Read the following סִדּוּר phrases. Circle God's name each time you read it.

1. אֲדֹנָי שְׂפָתַי תִּפְתָּח וּפִי יַגִּיד תְּהִלָּתֶךָ

2. בָּרוּךְ אַתָּה יְיָ נוֹתֵן הַתּוֹרָה

3. שְׁמַע יִשְׂרָאֵל יְהֹוָה אֱלֹהֵינוּ יְהֹוָה אֶחָד

4. אַתָּה גִבּוֹר לְעוֹלָם אֲדֹנָי

5. אַשְׁרֵי הָעָם שֶׁיְיָ אֱלֹהָיו

The סִדּוּר also has many additional names for God. Some of them are underlined below.
Read the following סִדּוּר phrases.

GOD	1	אֵל אָדוֹן עַל כָּל הַמַּעֲשִׂים
GOD	2	וַיְבָרֶךְ אֱלֹהִים אֶת יוֹם הַשְּׁבִיעִי
MY GOD	3	אֲרוֹמִמְךָ אֱלֹהַי הַמֶּלֶךְ
OUR GOD	4	בָּרוּךְ אַתָּה יְיָ אֱלֹהֵינוּ מֶלֶךְ הָעוֹלָם
GOD OF	5	אֱלֹהֵי אַבְרָהָם, אֱלֹהֵי יִצְחָק, וֵאלֹהֵי יַעֲקֹב

RULE #6

כָּל = כֹּל   Sometimes the vowel ָ is pronounced "OH."

מְאֹדֶךָ	וּבְכָל	נַפְשְׁךָ	וּבְכָל	1
וּבְשָׁכְבְּךָ	קָדְשְׁךָ	קָדְשׁוֹ	קֹדֶשׁ	2
חָפְשִׁי	עָבְדְּךָ	גָּדְלוֹ	אָזְנַיִם	3
שֶׁבְּכָל הַלֵּילוֹת	כָּל נִדְרֵי		עָזִּי	4

RULE #7

וֹ = ָ   The vowel ָ: is always pronounced "OH."

עֳמָרִים	חֳדָשִׁים	צֳפֳרִים	עֳנִי	אֳנִיָּה	1

RULE #8

צָהֳרַיִם   When the vowel ָ comes before the vowel ָ: in a word, both vowels are pronounced "OH."

פָּעֳלִי	צָהֳלָה	נָעֳמִי	מָחֳרַת	צָהֳרַיִם	אֳהָלִים	1

שְׁמַע/וְאָהַבְתָּ

1 שְׁמַע יִשְׂרָאֵל, יְיָ אֱלֹהֵינוּ, יְיָ אֶחָד.

2 בָּרוּךְ שֵׁם כְּבוֹד מַלְכוּתוֹ לְעוֹלָם וָעֶד.

3 וְאָהַבְתָּ אֵת יְיָ אֱלֹהֶיךָ

4 בְּכָל לְבָבְךָ וּבְכָל נַפְשְׁךָ וּבְכָל מְאֹדֶךָ.

5 וְהָיוּ הַדְּבָרִים הָאֵלֶה

6 אֲשֶׁר אָנֹכִי מְצַוְּךָ הַיּוֹם עַל לְבָבֶךָ.

7 וְשִׁנַּנְתָּם לְבָנֶיךָ וְדִבַּרְתָּ בָּם

8 בְּשִׁבְתְּךָ בְּבֵיתֶךָ וּבְלֶכְתְּךָ בַדֶּרֶךְ

9 וּבְשָׁכְבְּךָ וּבְקוּמֶךָ.

10 וּקְשַׁרְתָּם לְאוֹת עַל יָדֶךָ

11 וְהָיוּ לְטֹטָפֹת בֵּין עֵינֶיךָ.

12 וּכְתַבְתָּם עַל מְזֻזוֹת בֵּיתֶךָ וּבִשְׁעָרֶיךָ.

152

בִּרְכוֹת הַתּוֹרָה

1. בָּרְכוּ אֶת יְיָ הַמְבוֹרָךְ.

2. בָּרוּךְ יְיָ הַמְבוֹרָךְ לְעוֹלָם וָעֶד.

3. בָּרוּךְ אַתָּה יְיָ אֱלֹהֵינוּ מֶלֶךְ הָעוֹלָם,

4. אֲשֶׁר בָּחַר בָּנוּ מִכָּל הָעַמִּים

5. וְנָתַן לָנוּ אֶת תּוֹרָתוֹ.

6. בָּרוּךְ אַתָּה יְיָ נוֹתֵן הַתּוֹרָה.

1. בָּרוּךְ אַתָּה יְיָ אֱלֹהֵינוּ מֶלֶךְ הָעוֹלָם,

2. אֲשֶׁר נָתַן לָנוּ תּוֹרַת אֱמֶת

3. וְחַיֵּי עוֹלָם נָטַע בְּתוֹכֵנוּ.

4. בָּרוּךְ אַתָּה יְיָ נוֹתֵן הַתּוֹרָה.

וְזֹאת הַתּוֹרָה

1 וְזֹאת הַתּוֹרָה

2 אֲשֶׁר שָׂם מֹשֶׁה

3 לִפְנֵי בְּנֵי יִשְׂרָאֵל

4 עַל פִּי יְיָ בְּיַד מֹשֶׁה.

עֵץ חַיִּים הִיא

1 עֵץ חַיִּים הִיא לַמַּחֲזִיקִים בָּהּ

2 וְתֹמְכֶיהָ מְאֻשָּׁר

3 דְּרָכֶיהָ דַרְכֵי נֹעַם

4 וְכׇל נְתִיבוֹתֶיהָ שָׁלוֹם.

עָלֵינוּ

1 עָלֵינוּ לְשַׁבֵּחַ לַאֲדוֹן הַכֹּל

2 לָתֵת גְּדֻלָּה לְיוֹצֵר בְּרֵאשִׁית.

3 שֶׁלֹּא עָשָׂנוּ כְּגוֹיֵי הָאֲרָצוֹת

4 וְלֹא שָׂמָנוּ כְּמִשְׁפְּחוֹת הָאֲדָמָה...

5 וַאֲנַחְנוּ כּוֹרְעִים וּמִשְׁתַּחֲוִים וּמוֹדִים
   לִפְנֵי מֶלֶךְ מַלְכֵי הַמְּלָכִים,

6 הַקָּדוֹשׁ בָּרוּךְ הוּא...

7 וְנֶאֱמַר: וְהָיָה יְיָ לְמֶלֶךְ עַל כָּל הָאָרֶץ

8 בַּיּוֹם הַהוּא יִהְיֶה יְיָ אֶחָד וּשְׁמוֹ אֶחָד.

אֵין כֵּאלֹהֵינוּ

1	אֵין כֵּאלֹהֵינוּ	אֵין כַּאדוֹנֵינוּ
2	אֵין כְּמַלְכֵּנוּ	אֵין כְּמוֹשִׁיעֵנוּ.
3	מִי כֵאלֹהֵינוּ	מִי כַאדוֹנֵינוּ
4	מִי כְמַלְכֵּנוּ	מִי כְמוֹשִׁיעֵנוּ.
5	נוֹדֶה לֵאלֹהֵינוּ	נוֹדֶה לַאדוֹנֵינוּ
6	נוֹדֶה לְמַלְכֵּנוּ	נוֹדֶה לְמוֹשִׁיעֵנוּ.
7	בָּרוּךְ אֱלֹהֵינוּ	בָּרוּךְ אֲדוֹנֵינוּ
8	בָּרוּךְ מַלְכֵּנוּ	בָּרוּךְ מוֹשִׁיעֵנוּ.
9	אַתָּה הוּא אֱלֹהֵינוּ	אַתָּה הוּא אֲדוֹנֵינוּ
10	אַתָּה הוּא מַלְכֵּנוּ	אַתָּה הוּא מוֹשִׁיעֵנוּ.

מַה נִּשְׁתַּנָה

מַה נִּשְׁתַּנָה הַלַּיְלָה הַזֶּה מִכָּל הַלֵּילוֹת?

1 שֶׁבְּכָל הַלֵּילוֹת אָנוּ אוֹכְלִין
חָמֵץ וּמַצָּה. הַלַּיְלָה הַזֶּה כֻּלּוֹ מַצָּה.

2 שֶׁבְּכָל הַלֵּילוֹת אָנוּ אוֹכְלִין
שְׁאָר יְרָקוֹת. הַלַּיְלָה הַזֶּה מָרוֹר.

3 שֶׁבְּכָל הַלֵּילוֹת אֵין אָנוּ
מַטְבִּילִין אֲפִילוּ פַּעַם אֶחָת. הַלַּיְלָה
הַזֶּה שְׁתֵּי פְעָמִים.

4 שֶׁבְּכָל הַלֵּילוֹת אָנוּ אוֹכְלִין
בֵּין יוֹשְׁבִין וּבֵין מְסֻבִּין.
הַלַּיְלָה הַזֶּה כֻּלָּנוּ מְסֻבִּין.

הַתִּקְוָה

1 כֹּל עוֹד בַּלֵּבָב פְּנִימָה

2 נֶפֶשׁ יְהוּדִי הוֹמִיָּה,

3 וּלְפַאֲתֵי מִזְרָח קָדִימָה,

4 עַיִן לְצִיּוֹן צוֹפִיָּה;

5 עוֹד לֹא אָבְדָה תִּקְוָתֵנוּ,

6 הַתִּקְוָה בַּת שְׁנוֹת אַלְפַּיִם,

7 לִהְיוֹת עַם חָפְשִׁי בְּאַרְצֵנוּ,

8 אֶרֶץ צִיּוֹן וִירוּשָׁלַיִם.

WORD LIST – מִילוֹן

א

the first human, man	אָדָם
love	אַהֲבָה
God	אֱלֹהִים
Elijah the prophet	אֵלִיָּהוּ הַנָּבִיא
alef	אָלֶף
alef bet	אָלֶף בֵּית
amen	אָמֵן
truth	אֱמֶת
afikoman	אֲפִיקוֹמָן
the Holy Ark	אֲרוֹן הַקֹּדֶשׁ

ב

please	בְּבַקָשָׁה
bar mitzvah	בָּר מִצְוָה
praised, blessed	בָּרוּךְ
blessing	בְּרָכָה
daughter	בַּת
bat mitzvah	בַּת מִצְוָה

ה

havdalah, separation	הַבְדָּלָה
haggadah	הַגָּדָה
blessing over bread	הַמּוֹצִיא
Who brings forth bread	הַמּוֹצִיא לֶחֶם
Haftarah	הַפְטָרָה
the Merciful One (God)	הָרַחֲמָן
"The Hope", national anthem of Israel	הַתִּקְוָה

ו

and you shall love	וְאָהַבְתָּ

ח

happy holiday	חַג שָׂמֵחַ
live	חַי
challah, braided bread	חַלָּה
leavened food	חָמֵץ
Five Books of Moses	חֻמָשׁ
kindness	חֶסֶד

ט

tallit	טַלִּית

י

Jews	יְהוּדִים
holiday, festival	יוֹם טוֹב
Exodus from Egypt	יְצִיאַת מִצְרַיִם
Jerusalem	יְרוּשָׁלַיִם
moon	יָרֵחַ
Israel	יִשְׂרָאֵל

כ

bride	כַּלָּה
kippah, skullcap	כִּפָּה

ל

heart	לֵב
to life	לְחַיִּים

מ

scroll	מְגִלָּה
Shield of David, Jewish star	מָגֵן דָּוִד
mezuzah	מְזוּזָה
congratulations	מַזָּל טוֹב
machzor	מַחֲזוֹר
king, ruler	מֶלֶךְ
queen	מַלְכָּה
minyan, ten Jewish adults	מִנְיָן
matzah	מַצָּה
commandment	מִצְוָה
family	מִשְׁפָּחָה

נ

prophet	נָבִיא
soul	נֶפֶשׁ
eternal light	נֵר תָּמִיד

ס

prayer book	סִדּוּר
seder	סֵדֶר
Torah scroll, Five Books of Moses	סֵפֶר תּוֹרָה

ע

Hebrew	עִבְרִית
aliyah, going up	עֲלִיָּה
Tree of Life	עֵץ חַיִּים
Ten Commandments	עֲשֶׂרֶת הַדִּבְּרוֹת

פ

Passover	פֶּסַח

צ

justice	צְדָקָה
fringes on tallit	צִיצִית

ק

Welcoming Shabbat	קַבָּלַת שַׁבָּת
Kiddush	קִדּוּשׁ
holy	קָדוֹשׁ
Kaddish	קַדִּישׁ

ר

Jewish New Year	רֹאשׁ הַשָּׁנָה

שׁ

Shabbat	שַׁבָּת
the Sabbath Bride	שַׁבָּת הַכַּלָּה
the Sabbath Queen	שַׁבָּת הַמַּלְכָּה
a peaceful Shabbat	שַׁבָּת שָׁלוֹם
shofar	שׁוֹפָר
hello, goodbye, peace	שָׁלוֹם
Rejoicing of the Torah	שִׂמְחַת תּוֹרָה
hear	שְׁמַע
helper	שַׁמָּשׁ
Happy New Year	שָׁנָה טוֹבָה

ת

Torah, teaching	תּוֹרָה
prayer	תְּפִלָּה

אָלֶף בֵּית

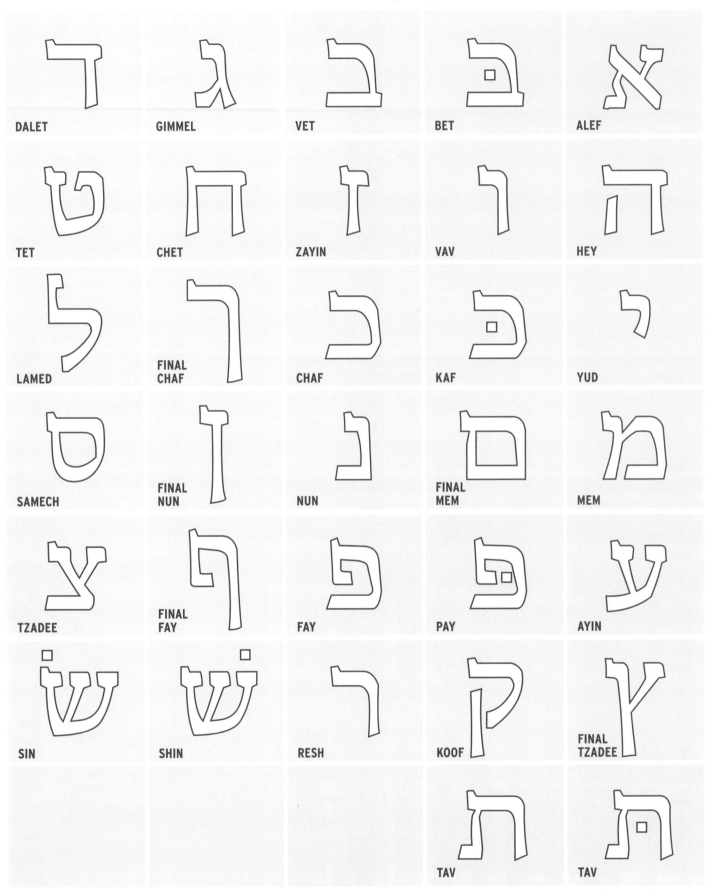

DALET	GIMMEL	VET	BET	ALEF
TET	CHET	ZAYIN	VAV	HEY
LAMED	FINAL CHAF	CHAF	KAF	YUD
SAMECH	FINAL NUN	NUN	FINAL MEM	MEM
TZADEE	FINAL FAY	FAY	PAY	AYIN
SIN	SHIN	RESH	KOOF	FINAL TZADEE
			TAV	TAV